Gaining a Little Altitude

Leaving Ideology on the Ground

Robert V. Wills

Lemon Lane Press • Santa Ana, California

Lemon Lane Press
1811 Beverly Glen Drive
Santa Ana, CA 92705
(714) 544-0344

www.maralys.com

Cover & book design: Sue Campbell
Cover photo of Everest at dawn: Bernard Goldbach
Interior photo of Everest: Luca Galuzzi — www.galuzzi.it

Printed in the United States of America

Praise for *Gaining a Little Altitude*

Bob Wills' series of essays in *Gaining a Little Altitude* make fascinating reading. His insightful and timely essays cover a spectrum of topics from the political and economic state of the planet to the social and ethical systems of the day. Thought-provoking ... they're worth your time.

William Kropp, Ph.D.,
Research physicist

Prepare to have your lapels grabbed by this pithy volume! You'll find opinionated, witty, thought-provoking perspectives generated by a razor-sharp intellect focused on politics, the human condition, and the future of our country and our world.

Jevelyn Yonchar, M.D.

Well-written and researched, sometimes reflective and melancholic, often direct and audacious, always intelligent and thought-provoking, his essays, for a moment, stop me in my tracks. Make me think. Make me wonder. Make me say out loud: Amen!

Bernardine Wilcox, M.P.T.

After years of hearing this brilliant lawyer's wisdom and insights, I'm happy to see it down on paper for all of us to share. A treat to read an original viewpoint.

Elaine Weinberg, J.D.

Robert Wills' essays are consistently thought-provoking, covering a wide and varied range of subjects. His writing style is succinct and compelling. Based on the author's life experiences, and coupled with his wide range of knowledge and quick recall of facts, the essays always ring true. I eagerly await each new one!

Linda R. Mayeda, M.A.

Only Bob Wills, a lawyer with his own law firm, could write the book, *Lawyers Are Killing America*, and make it convincing as well as fascinating. I couldn't put it down. Wills often sees how the nation or the world must change, and makes a case which convinces and captures the reader. Bob's essays are also a winner.

Allan Klumpp, M.A.
Engineer
Apollo Lunar Descent Guidance

Gaining a Little Altitude gives the reader a look into the mind of a great thinker. Bob's thoughts on young and old, red and blue, small pleasures and great calamities, are a gift to behold. With his mixture of sharp prose and just plain common sense, you will find yourself savoring these essays, and thinking of them long after you've finished this book.

Beth Strayer Handweiler, C.S.R.

Contents

Acknowledgements

Show me a wordsmith and I'll show you someone who doesn't suffer editing lightly. The fact that I allowed Maralys to tinker a bit with some of my sentences in these pieces is no testimony to my good nature. Rather, it's a tribute to her evolved skill as an editor and manuscript polisher. And a payback for some of the nuggets I've planted in her fifteen books....

Maralys also runs the computer in this house and got my prose to the printer in apple pie order. So she gets double points for editing and production.

Brad Hagen gets one Brownie point for buying an Alpha Smart keyboard for Maralys, only because I commandeered it and do all my writing on it.

Allene Symons was a peach in turning out my first volume of essays, *A View From The Hill.* She's also a brilliant editor and publisher.

Sue Campbell provided invaluable design and production for this second little volume of essays. She knows more about book design and production than we will ever know and we are grateful for her help.

Foreword

The Golden Years aren't always golden, but retirement does offer a few bonuses.

Since I dissolved my law firm and sold our office building, I've had more time to reflect on the passing parade and record some critical impressions. Hopefully, having gathered eight decades of memories and having lived in diverse habitats and work environments has enhanced my perspective. It's probably not a coincidence that my degrees come in three diverse fields of study, and that my professional career ranged from corporate counsel, to medical malpractice trial attorney, to securities investor. And that our travels have ranged over four continents.

Any reader other than a friend or relative will soon find it difficult to believe that I am still registered as a Republican in Orange County, because I share so few views with 21st Century Republicans—and my disgust with them since Reagan is so explicit. Since politics is so pervasive in modern American life, I don't see how anyone examining his own life or his society can ignore it for long.

And I haven't.

So in today's polarized society, I have to warn any red-white-and-blue, God-fearing, card-carrying member of the Grand Old Party to proceed further with caution lest he or she take my views as a personal assault. Or suffer the same epiphany that I did when, in the early 1980s, the Gipper became the hallowed leader of the Free World.

Aside from American politics, I hope that my forays into ethics, sociology, and philosophy do cover a wider range of vantage points than average and that my crystal ball isn't too cloudy. I threw away my rose-colored glasses about 40 years ago, and wonder if any cockeyed optimist today is in touch with reality.

Meanwhile, thanks for dropping by.

Robert V. Wills

Part 1

Is America Ripe for Revolution?

THERE ARE TWO ELEMENTS of American society that could converge in a few years and set the stage for a violent upheaval having all the earmarks of a revolution. It would be the third since 1776. And it would kill a lot of innocent people, as all revolutions do.

I don't mean local riots. I don't mean sit-ins or demonstrations or parades. I don't mean occupying. I mean armed insurrection.

The two predisposing elements are a growing and unhealthy disparity in the distribution of American wealth and a growing ethnic underclass that has neither faith in nor allegiance to democracy.

There is probably enough anger and ignorance in the underclass to fuel an armed insurrection. And God knows there are enough guns, bullets, and explosives afoot in the American underworld to arm them. But what the disaffected lack, and could not proceed without, is an articulate and charismatic leader, a Martin Luther King with napalm in his rhetoric and racial unrest instead of scripture in his message. He would have to be Bobby Kennedy with both a torch and a grenade. He would have to be Jesus Christ marching on the temples.

Your first reaction is that it can't happen here. We don't have a monarchy. We have a huge, spread out country. We have a military that could meet any violent challenge. We don't have a clearly defined target of a revolution. No czar. No Louis XIV. No Khadaffi. No Mubarak. No Chiang Kai Shek. No Ceauşescu.

True enough. The target needs definition. Who do they overthrow? You can't target and attack the infamous 1 percent elite — that's three and a half million people scattered far and wide. You can't pillage Wall Street and Manhattan, or K Street and Capitol Hill. The billionaires are located all over the place, from Maine to Florida to Texas to Hawaii. And the billionaires don't make the rules that got them fat and elevated in the first place — that is the fallout of politicians and administrators and executives.

So even if the angry mobs of disaffected have-nots could ever get articulate and dedicated leadership, then recruit thousands of armed rebels, who and where would they attack? Probably the White House and the congress, and maybe the Stock Exchange and headquarters of some of the biggest banks in New York. But how long would those skirmishes last when embattled government leaders call up the Army, Marines, and

National Guard from innumerable locations?

No, I'm afraid the political and physical institution we know as the U.S. is too big to overthrow by armed conflict from within. A monarchy or dictatorship has an identifiable and localized target. The U.S. is simply too big and too scattered and too diversified to uproot. The disaffected and the deprived can raise only a media ruckus and political discussion through localized violent attacks.

Ask The Unabomber and Timothy McVeigh and the Watts rioters, the Detroit arsonists, The Branch Davidians, the Montana Freemen, the "Sovereign" wackos. Ask the Students for a Democratic Society, the Symbionese Liberation Army, and the Black Panthers. Then ask the Occupiers how much hope peaceful demonstrations have for changing the American economy and tax code.

As I contemplate the task of organizing a third American revolution, I'm led to the conclusion that, at least for the near future, violent attacks on the U.S. institution will generate only media coverage — grist for the evening news — and political commentary of limited duration. The only route to change in the U.S. economy is through change at the top, meaning the White House, the Senate, and the House. They make the laws, define the taxes, distribute the wealth (in the future, at least), and appoint the judges to police their efforts. Likewise in the fifty states. The Governor's

Office and the Legislature set the rules for the future and appoint the judges.

If there is going to be any redistribution of wealth in this country, the executive and legislative branches will engineer it — or ignore it.

So, in contemplating whether the U.S. is ripe for revolution, I've given up the ghost. It isn't. The angry and the disaffected, the deprived and the abused, won't be able to get organized and anoint a leader for the assault. I see no hope for anything but disruptions, incidents, news stories, and editorials. In the end the only weapon an American revolutionary has is, ironically, the basic weapon of democracy. The ballot box. Vote the bad ones out. And tell the new ones what you want.

Tell them to rewrite the Internal Revenue Code. Tell them to do what's right for the greatest number, not what their campaign contributors have paid for. And start out by passing new laws limiting the scope and power of campaign contributors. They and their lobbyists are the reason we've gotten to the point where we are even asking ourselves about a third American revolution....

1/27/12

Life Goes On. And On. And On.

A**nd Rarely Looks Back.**
Our family room wall is both a museum and a mausoleum. The den wall, too. The plaques, trophies, and photos speak of vigor, dynamism, triumph, and glory. The plaques and trophies bespeak triumph, excellence, and status, in five sports, some on a world or national level. The photos reflect confidence, pride, and robustness. Wow! What a bunch! What a record. What a life....

But the trophies and photos need periodic dusting. Some of the photos are fading a bit with time. The dates all fell in the last century ... The entire display, like all trophy cases, photo albums, memorials, and statues represents lives and events frozen in time; time past, time never to return. The tennis phenoms, swimming stars, and hang gliding champions all moved on, grew older, moved away. Two even died. And we who remain are stiffened by arthritis and weathered by time. The few new photos are large, multi-generational groups at plush water holes or in transit. There are no new trophies or plaques, not for 35 years....

The parade is over and the crowd has gone home. We are the only two left in the stands, leafing through the program. It was a great parade. Exciting. Dramatic. And it was a fairly long one. But all that's left are the program, the photos, and the memories. All around us life goes on without so much as a pause. There are new parades and new trophies and new triumphs for the new teams. The bright young faces on our walls are now filling their own walls and trophy cases from different venues and different arenas.

And thus far, despite our trappings, we have been wise enough not to bury ourselves in reminiscence and nostalgia. They are more the road to depression and remorse than to repose or gratification. The past was great, but the past is past. The Bard rightly said, let the dead past bury its dead. But if the past was truly great surely a memorial is in order, if not a shrine.

The present is insistent and demanding. And not all bad. But the past sure had its great moments. And they aren't forgotten here, on our walls at least....

6/22/12

Isn't it Lonely Being an Only?

I'VE BEEN ASKED ON occasion whether I missed having a brother or a sister growing up, whether I felt isolated or lonely as an only child. The question always took me aback, for several reasons.

In the first place, I always basked in the sense that I was the top dog, even though I was the only dog. An only child is number one in every sense, and gathers all of the attention and good efforts of both parents. (I was lucky enough to have two parents focused on me, ill-mated though they were, and was never the object of child-rearing conflict). Had I been raised by a single parent in straightened circumstances, I might have welcomed some sibling company. But the disparity between Art Wills and Ruth Wills concerned money and monogamy, not my performance level or best interests.

The other factors that made me ponder the question involve sibling rivalry, sibling conflict, and parental favoritism. I see so many cases of frosty — or shattered — sibling relationships I wonder how I would have fared with a sibling with an equally strong personality. Or how I would have responded to any shade of parental favoritism. Not well, I'm sure.

Then I contemplate what I regard as the bonus a single child receives, not only of attention and resources, but of the self-reliance and independence that being solo produces. I've always regarded solitude and isolation as a form of luxury, largely because I run my own life and make my own rules. I can focus on my project without interference, my performance without local competition. I have to rely on myself and soon enough decide that I am the most reliable.

I think it's easier for an only to develop both a strong case of self-reliance and a strong sense of self-worth because of it. In fact, I think that most psychological profiles of children reveal that single children score higher in self-reliance and self-esteem than children with siblings. And I'm sure we score lower in social interaction and social skills.

I have a suspicion that many siblings secretly envy their solo counterparts, free as they are of all that conflict and competition. But those who cherish close relations with their siblings might not — and are probably the ones who ask me the question, "Don't you get lonely as an only?"....

7/7/12

Why, Really, Do They Abhor The "R" Word?

How cynical do you have to be to ask why the Republicans shrink in dread when they hear anything about regulation? Is it only because they think that regulation puts a brake on the free flow of energy and innovation? That it clogs the free market? That it depresses initiative? That is dampens the human spirit? That it takes away a God-given right to freedom of action?

Sorry ... not! It's a lot more mundane and mercenary than that. The right wing associates regulation with Big Brother, 1984, and that nastiest of bugaboos, socialism. It means restraints, red tape, bureaucracy, surveillance, oversight, arbitrary and capricious tyranny. In short, an unholy and dangerous choke hold on freedom of action by the almighty individual.

But it's not the danger to the human spirit that spurs lobbyists and Republican politicians into action whenever a bill that includes some form of the "R" word is in committee. It's the danger to the P&L statement, the bottom line, the cash flow, the profits. It raises the specter of increasing costs or limiting profits, whether through adding personnel or processes or setting prices. Manufacturers like factories and power plants fight processes and equipment designed to increase safety or reduce environmental damage. Retailers resist wage regulations — minimum wage, overtime, child labor, and maximum hour rules — special needs facilities, and price controls (the ultimate being public utilities).

Financial institutions like banks and insurance companies fight restrictions on trading, type of business activities, and rates (Glass-Steagall, Dodd-Frank, usury laws, rate regulations). We have endless Federal and State alphabet agencies FTC, SEC, FCC, FAA, NLRB, FDIC, FSLIC, FDA, FHA, FRB, USDA ad infinitum) regulating — or theoretically regulating — major areas of our lives, far too many to suit Libertarians and Republicans.

But we still have a scandal a week involving unscrupulous opportunists working either outside government regulation or through the endless loopholes and exceptions inserted in legislation through the efforts of lobbyists and anti-regulation politicians. We are as swamped by sleazy con artists, scammers, and plunderers today as we are by a patchwork of leaky regulations.

The fact of the matter is that we need more

regulation, or better regulation — or a surge in individual morality in the American population. I'm not holding my breath on an ethical revival, not in this lifetime or this culture. Nor would I bank on congress or Sacramento getting its act together on genuine, balanced regulation. So I guess for now the motto will have to be: caveat emptor and by all means avoid swimming with the sharks....

7/16/12

Even The Air You Breathe....

I T's DEAD EASY TO agree with the millions of Americans who are thoroughly disgusted with the American political system. The sophisticated among them know that the political process reaches all the way down from the U.S. Supreme Court to the Tustin City Council. And most of the skeptics share a sense of fatalism because they don't think there is anything they can do about the mess.

But being repulsed by American politics doesn't justify a lack of interest or some degree of participation. Those disgusting politicians ultimately control almost every detail of our lives, the roads we travel, the food we eat, even the air we breathe. Whether we are a one percenter or a recluse, there is no aspect of our lives that isn't affected by the votes in legislative or judicial chambers — or the lack of votes therein. You don't have to be a demographer, meteorologist, chemist, or epidemiologist to discern the relationship between political activity and overpopulation, global warming, air quality, food safety, property development, cost of living.

When so-called conservatives defund revenue for family planning, birth control, and sex education, they directly impact population trends which in turn exacerbate all the other resource and environmental problems. When they defund PBS and CPB and NEA, they threaten the quality of life for millions of art and culture lovers. And when the other side of the aisle increases the regulation of commerce and development, they discourage or burden entrepreneurial activity. It isn't just the power to tax that is the power to destroy. It's the power to legislate or the judicial power to annul that is the power to destroy — or to remedy.

So how can anyone who cares about his country, his community, and his family turn his back on the political system that regulates all of it — and actually determines his future? Drought and famine, floods and earthquakes, wild fires and volcanic eruptions may come and go. They can't be outlawed by politicians. But we now have the science to know that, except for earthquakes and volcanic eruptions, the votes — or lack of votes — by those politicians we denigrate can make a difference in our lives, or at least the lives of our descendants.

So if you are that disgusted but you care at all about the future of your kids and grandkids, you should do more than just cast one vote every two years. Support your party and some good candidates (hopefully not ones like the amateur ideologues now populating the

House). Write a few checks; money does sway the ignorant segment of the electorate. But most of all let part of the world know how you feel. Instead of holding forth on the weather or the latest celebrity or disaster, make your own campaign speech or conduct your own poll.

But duck if you're talking to a confirmed enemy ideologue....

7/20/12

WOULD THE FRAMERS TOLERATE MASSACRES?

IN 1789 THEY HAD long, slow-loading, one-shot muskets. The pistols were single-shot devices suitable for dueling. Neither was accurate at more than a short distance. They had no concept of automatic weapons, assault rifles, machine guns, or other weapons of rapid mass homicide. There were no gun shops or Internet gun deals.

The Second Amendment to the Constitution was part of the Bill of Rights, adopted in 1789, two years after the Constitution itself was adopted. It asserted that a "well-regulated Militia" was "necessary to the security of a free state" so that "the right of the people to keep and bear arms shall not be infringed." That language, drafted 223 years ago, raises two questions of definition.

First, what was a "Militia" as conceived in 1789? Webster's today defines it as "an army of citizens who are not soldiers by profession, called up in time of emergency." It must have had pretty much the same meaning in 1789; Article II, Section 2 of the Constitution refers to the President as the "Commander in Chief of the Army and Navy of the United States," so the use of the term "Militia" obviously meant a separate citizens' army. The document is silent on who could call up a Militia or keep it "well-regulated."

But the framers obviously conceived a group of private citizens who could produce their own "arms" when called up, since "the people" were given the right to "keep and bear arms," obviously meaning their personal arms. Therefore, the key word in the Second Amendment when it comes to the question of regulating weapons is the word "arms" itself. Is a nuclear device a form of "arms"? Probably not, if congress has anything to say about it. Is a 105mm. Howitzer the kind of "arms" the people can "keep and bear"? How about a usable chemical weapon, like mustard gas or ricin? … And, finally, how about hand grenades and automatic weapons with extended cartridge clips?

None of those modern weapons were in existence in 1789. Or conceived. So did the framers mean "arms" of every type or concept, real or imagined? Or did they intend to cover only "arms" known and extant in 1789?

Probably the latter. It's doubtful that American colonists would ever have sanctioned a civilian citizen, aged 18 or aged 60, sane or unbalanced, model citizen or ex-con, keeping and bearing a weapon that can fire 100 rounds in one minute, or even 8 rounds in 5 seconds (like my M-1). Or purchasing by mail or Internet enough ammo to arm a small Militia himself.

From 1994 to 2004 it was illegal for a private citizen to purchase an assault weapon in the U.S. That Federal statute was never successfully challenged in Court. How the present Supreme Court would rule on it is unknown, since the Court is as political and ideological as congress. But if congress ever gets the courage to impose some controls on automatic weapons, five of the Supremes would have a hard time ruling that in 1789 the word "arms" was meant to include weapons of mass destruction or mass annihilation, like assault weapons.

But the chance of a court ruling on the scope and intent of the Second Amendment is slim to none. Most Republicans are card-carrying members of the NRA, one of Washington's two most deadly lobbies. And most Democrats are too worried about reelection and too afraid of the NRA "Kill List" to vote for gun control and get on that list....

The gun lobby preaches that our precious American freedom requires that gun ownership be unfettered except in the case of convicts or certified psychos. They argue that, since the framers offered no definition of "arms" and imposed no limits on quantities or types of "arms," there should be no limits. Then they add their old saw, "with gun control only criminals will have guns," blithely ignoring the hundreds of millions of guns already in the hands of non-criminals.

So on with the assault weapon massacres in the hands of angry, unbalanced Americans. Let freedom ring — as the shots ring out....

7/23/12

A Salutary Friend at the End...

You don't normally pick your friends like you pick a contractor, repairman, or financial adviser — by reputation, word of mouth, or advertisement. Your friends come by way of proximity, like neighbors or classmates or fellow employees. They come through association in clubs, organizations, church. They come because of common interests or common problems. They last because you have things in common and enjoy each other's company.

Your doctor, lawyer, broker, accountant, or repairman may become a friend, but not initially because of their trade or profession. His or her friendship may impart some collateral counsel or assistance as you go through life, but you may be especially fortunate if your good friend is a respected physician. Because the closer you get to the end of your journey the more medical issues and medical skills are going to pervade your daily life, probably escalating to the dominant factor in your very existence. Unless you are one of the supposedly fortunate individuals who check out with sudden death syndrome (a massive occlusion of the left anterior descending coronary artery),or a massive hemorrhagic stroke, or a ruptured aneurysm, your terminal and end stage will be controlled by physicians. Not executives or CPA's or financial advisers or lawyers or clergy or best friends, but physicians. That is, unless you're foolish enough to be in an HMO, in which case you may depart in the middle of a debate between bean counters and physicians....

It's a fact of life that only the gravely ill, the critically ill, and their physicians realize that the final chapter of most people's lives will unavoidably be consumed by medical problems and medical decisions.

That's when the best gatekeeper and consultant you can have is a knowledgeable, well-respected member of the local medical community — a doctor. That's when you need advice from someone who really cares — and knows the system. That's when the "Obamacare" hater discovers that the medical system of the great United States is indeed dysfunctional, if not broken That's when you come to see that America really does have a stratified, split-level pool of medical care, the best in the world for the well-heeled and connected, a low fat version for the HMO's and military services, and a third world level for the poor.

We still have the best doctors in the world, but you need a good medical policy, a rare case, or a friend to get treated by the very best. We have legions of competent physicians on the staffs of our local hospitals, but no way for the unsophisticated layman to winnow them out of the herd — except word of mouth from friends, the Internet, or, God forbid, advertisements.

Having represented and deposed and cross-examined doctors for 27 years, as a medical malpractice attorney, I got to know the difference between the good ones and the mediocre, or downright incompetent. I developed a great admiration for the good ones and real sympathy for those abused by our tort system (a litigation lottery where the client doesn't even have to buy a ticket).

If you're in the so-called golden years and still in the pink, you can thank both your genetic forebears and American medicine (or at the least, American epidemiology). Our ancestors didn't live nearly this long, or this well. But one of these days you'll need some excellent medical care to extend your stay. And it will help your case if you count a doctor or two among your friends and relatives. That kind of a friend when you're in need can truly be a friend indeed.

7/27/12

The Cold Snap and the Silent Woman: How Feckless Males Get Frostbite.

It's a fortunate young man who hasn't had at least one target of his youthful passion freeze up and silently walk away from the partnership. If he hasn't had that experience, it's because he's a precocious lover who plays a woman's body like a musical instrument. Or because he hasn't yet found a young woman who inspired and allowed intimacy.

The fact is that healthy young males are 1)charged with passion, 2)confident beyond their abilities, 3) unschooled in the intricacies of the female anatomy, 4) slow learners, and 5) driven by burning passion to a hasty explosion of ardor.

Instead of asking, "Is this all there is?," or suggesting that the clumsy swain go to school about erotic pleasures, the female is most apt to cool off precipitously without explanation and put a silent "hold" on the relationship. She may not even identify the cause of her disaffection in her own conscious mind — the female psyche is complex and a quality woman likes to think of herself as sweet and wholesome and kind. It might seem bestial on her part to banish a lover for sexual deficiency alone, but the timing of the icy disenchantment speaks louder than her conscious rationalization. Or her explanation to friends.

All of this assumes that the disenchanted female was not repulsed by bad breath, body odor, bad manners, bad breeding, lack of ambition, or lack of IQ ... I suspect there are sources of dispassion other than inadequate or clumsy love–making. But if the cold snap set in immediately after youthful intercourse, don't rule out my theory too hastily....

8/19/12

It Isn't Smart to Look Bored.

Is it just me, or is most social conversation inane? I'm increasingly being accused of being detached and non-conversational, presumably because I'm seriously deaf. It's true — I do miss a lot of table talk because I miss words, especially if there is more than one conversation in progress, which is almost always the case with groups of six or more. The other problem is that I hear conversations on my left, even at an adjoining table, much better than one on my right. And in a group of eight or more, which seems to inspire three or more conversations at once, I semi-automatically tune out all chatter and wish I was somewhere else, like at a table for two in a quiet restaurant.

But the problem is more complex than that. I guess I can blame the deafness for seeming withdrawn in a group, but a more basic cause is, dare I say the word, boredom. Am I getting smarter in my senility or are most people getting more vapid in their commentary? I doubt the former, so suspect the latter. Make a mental note sometime of the topics covered in conversation with friends and relatives. If you can avoid the weather, the latest scandal, the grandkids, the medical ailments (organ recital), and the vacation trip, you are lucky. But did you learn anything of value? Or anything new?

Maybe I'm being silly. Since when is social intercourse supposed to be educational? Why should a chat be instructional? But how long can an over-the-fence exchange go on before it gets banal and becomes a time waster? How are you? How was your day? Is anyone so hungry for recognition they welcome ice-breakers like that?

Not me, that's for sure. It's all I can do to avoid a sarcastic response to those openers. ("Which organ system shall we start with?," "Do you want the good news or the bad breaks first?")

Admittedly, cheery greetings and ice-breakers are intended only to say hello, good to see you. A stony stare or reflexive grunt would be taken as a sign of rude disinterest, if not hostility. So the encounter must start with tradition and platitudes. "Hi, how are you?" isn't supposed to open an exchange. It's just "Hi."

What happens after that is what either enlivens, enlightens, or bores. No one ever declares, "I have nothing to report," or I'm not in the mood to chat." And if the meeting is at a social gathering or a dinner table, some level of conversation is mandatory. And only on Masterpiece Theater does the gracious host take the lead in an orderly, one-at-a-time discussion. And only in our discussion group do we have a rule that one person speaks at a time, so everyone can listen. And only in court could I count on being the only speaker on the floor at one time.

I miss that aspect of the courtroom. We don't have *Masterpiece Theater* type of dinners in 2012 Orange County. And discussion group meets only once a month.

So I'm stuck with multiple-discussion dinner meetings and family gatherings. In this family, a gathering resembles an Irish Parliament, where everyone talks at once. And my voice is no longer the loudest… So I'm going to have to look interested in even the most vapid discussions. And to smile and nod even if I don't know — or care — what they're talking about. The fact is, my disinterest, often boredom, is starting to show. And people resent boredom when they are holding forth. Even more than they resent arrogance if you challenge some of their ridiculous assertions.…

8/24/12

Footnote: Oh my God, it's déjà vu all over again. Since penning the above soliloquy, I've run across my high school yearbook. And here's what they wrote about me 68 years ago, in 1944:

"This fellow sees me through, although he would not have me know it. He'd rather have men call him dumb than embarrass me and show it."

Is Yankee America Dead?

M Y GRANDKIDS WOULDN'T EVEN recognize the America I grew up in. For them it would be like visiting a Scottish hamlet or an Austrian village, a homogeneous population with traditional values. Faces were white and families were definitive. No single parents absent a recent death. Entertainment consisted of the AM radio, puzzles and games, and what would be G rated movies. Boy Scouts and FFA and church groups thrived. The County Fair was very special, as were Easter, Halloween, and Christmas.

It was essentially an Anglo-Saxon society. English, Irish, Welsh, German, French roots. The one Jewish family usually owned a store, a market or an outlet. Italians were OK, easily identified, considered jolly and athletic — and Catholic.

There were no Hispanic or made up given names, because there were no Hispanics or blacks. The social center was the Protestant, usually Congregational, church. There was a "village idiot" and a few kids with learning disabilities. The ones with severe disability weren't visible. They were in "insane asylums" or "special homes." I doubt that there were "divorcée" lawyers; I recall no known case of divorce among our acquaintances.

Country schools had more than one grade in a classroom. My small hamlet had all eight grades in one room, with one teacher…(I still remember her name, and the fact I was a good speller). After school activity consisted of picking wild berries, feeding the chickens, and trout fishing in Big Branch or Otter Creek. In my case it was mostly trout watching; I could never get that big Eastern Brook in Otter Creek to bite … Other kids had real farm chores. For a little while I was lucky enough to have an ex-Cavalry riding horse in the barn.

The big news while we lived in that little Vermont hamlet was the 1936 coronation of King George VI and the 1937 crash of the Hindenburg. No TV — just radio coverage and newspaper photos … without TV you can imagine how long those cold winter evenings were. And what a big deal *Snow White and The Seven Dwarfs* was at the Paramount Theater in Rutland.

Life was obviously a lot simpler in the thirties. A Coke or a candy bar was a nickel. So was a phone call or a newspaper. There was no AIDS, MRSA, SARS, Ebola, Lyme Disease, or West Nile Virus. All we worried about were mumps, measles, whooping cough, and scarlet fever. Polio was a distant scare in warmer climates.

Homosexuals were deep in the closet. Gay Pride wasn't even on the horizon. Single sex marriage hadn't even been conceived. Lesbians were only in avant garde literature. Pedophilia wasn't even in the vocabulary. The Catholic Church was sacrosanct. The newspapers relished an occasional murder. Birth control consisted of abstinence or 7Up douches....

Oh yes, it was quite a different world before WWII ... I doubt that our grandkids could even imagine a world with no TV, no computers, no Internet, no cell phones, no R rated movies, and only one family car — with no seat belts, no turn signals, no electric windows or door locks, and no baby seats.

The years in Mt. Tabor, Vermont were followed by three years in Vermont's second largest city, Rutland. A city of 17,000 wasn't exactly urban, and I was still able to have a few chickens and sell eggs. But there were lots of Wills ventures out of WASP society in those years. Once the snow flew, my restless mother took me out of school on junkets to Miami, Panama, and even California (on the Panama Pacific Line). There was brief schooling in Miami, the Canal Zone, and Los Angeles, but only long enough to develop tales to tell the class back in Rutland. (The teacher would have me stand up in front and report....) Panama and Havana were exotic enough for an eleven year old country boy, but the big adventure was a trip with Rutland Boy Scouts to camp at the World's Fair in New York in

1940. That was really big time....

Then skipping grade eight in Winchester, a tony Boston suburb, was a challenge, especially since a Vermont country boy was starting his Freshman year at Winchester High School a month or two late. By the time I got adjusted to that fast track, we were headed west — goodbye New England forever — to Long Beach, California, because my dad had been transferred from Boston Navy Yard to Hawaii. I finished ninth grade at Franklin Jr. High in Long Beach. The rest of my adolescence is another story, involving Pearl Harbor, herding cows and feeding trout in Montana, toting suitcases in Sequoia Park, and starring (academically at least), in military school in Carlsbad, California.

Fast forward seventy years to Orange County in 2012. As I watch the roiling masses on TV, go to a concert, survey the crowd at Souplantation and Costco, then meet the friends and classmates of my grandkids and great grandkids, I silently ask myself, "Where is the America I grew up in? Where did all the white people go? Why is every football or basketball player brown or black? How many languages am I listening to at Costco and Souplantation? Why does every TV ad have to have a black or Asian in it? Why is every movie and TV cast unavoidably multiracial?"

Don't tighten up. Don't recoil. Don't pull out the "R" card. Don't roll your eyes. It's OK. A colorama culture isn't all that bad. I can adjust to a rainbow coalition.

It just takes time. And I don't like it pushed in my face. That white Yankee society wasn't all that bad. Because it was MY society — better than anything I've seen since in Central or South America. Or Africa. Or Asia. Maybe the Technicolor global techno-society will be a better one. I hope so. But as far as I'm concerned, the jury is still out. Only time will tell.

P.S. Eighty years ago Barack Obama would not have been welcome in Yankee America. That would have been America's loss then, and it will be America's huge loss today if white America replaces him with Romney next month....

9/27/12

Fast Eyes and Nimble Brains?

IF YOU WANT TO see how flittery and twitchy our techno-society has become, just watch my TV screen any weekday morning. The program is CNBC in high definition, which gives me a wider screen than standard CNBC. The wider screen gives several additional panels of business data, so that at any one time, there are no fewer than six panels or strips of information, most flipping after five or six seconds, all surrounding the central commentator or chart in the center of the screen.

The NYSE and NASDAQ "tapes" are rolling across the bottom of the screen, right to left. They give the stock, the stock symbol, and the latest trade figure. They alone would keep your eyes rolling constantly if you follow the trades.

Then there is a line of other business data across the top of the screen, giving five or six key indicators. It flips every five seconds, so you have to be a fast reader up there, too.

Then the panel on the right ("Biz Briefs" or

"Market Pulse" or "Chart Smarts" or "Scorecard") has text squibs and charts — lasting anywhere from three to eight seconds. Below them is a panel showing coming attractions for later today. It flips every six or seven seconds. Then below that is a running digital clock — "Closing Bell" time remaining.

The main picture, often a panel of regulars and guests, fills the left bulk of the screen, but it too superimposes a lot of charts and data reflecting their topic. And in the lower right corner of that is another flipping display of key indexes, the Dow, NASDAQ, gold, oil, bond interest, etc.

The only relief from the dazzling jumble of figures and squibs is the ads, which tend to sweep the screen of all data and slow the pace to a "clever, sincere, casual, or heartfelt" portrait. That lasts on average 12 to 15 seconds, but is usually a fast series of images. Once again, no one image stays on screen more than a few seconds.

I suspect that my CNBC screen is really just the quintessence of modern American society. Sound bytes and multitasking reflect the faster cadence of Generation Y. But how many people's eyes can cover six or seven bytes of data in three or four seconds, or read text fast enough to flip all over a wide screen in seconds? And how many brains can process that stream of sound bytes ad "sight bytes"?*

To add to the bedlam I keep the channel on mute

because I'm interested in the data and not the blather. But if the discussion does touch on an area of interest to me, I have to add the caption text to the other text, and the eyes have to flit around even faster.

The question the psychologists and neurologists are reportedly now working on is whether the sound byte, "sight byte," and multitasking pace is either changing or overtaxing the Generation Y brain. I've always been a fast reader, but the twitchy pace challenges at least one "Greatest Generation" brain....

10/3/12

*"Sight byte" first used by Maralys K. Wills on 10/3/12.

A SHINING BEACON OF HOPE

WATCHING VIOLENT STREET MOBS, armed conflict, and "ultimate" combat on TV makes me wonder about the prospects for homo sapiens. Watching the slimy hypocrisy of GOP politicians like Bush and Romney does the same. As long as we have live TV and investigative journalism, it's hard not to become a real cynic in the good old USA.

But watching a hundred or so college musicians play Beethoven's "Leonore Overture" and Tchaikovsky's "Fourth Symphony" last night — play them as well as the major symphony orchestras we see in the Performing Arts Center — restored a little bit of my confidence in our future. These are demanding compositions and I know them well from my classical music listening years. The strings played flawlessly, even the pizzicato movement, and the horns, woodwinds, and percussion were incredible in pieces where any blue note would stand out. I can't believe that a bunch of 2012 "kids" could meld together in the intricacy, discipline, and coordination required by those and two other pieces.

That hour and a half of skill, dedication, and finesse was the exact antithesis of the bedlam and mayhem we see daily on network TV. The standing ovation at the climactic close of conductor Kimo Furumoto's Sunday afternoon performance was evidence that there is still hope for America's youth — or some of them.

My enjoyment of the two pieces and the "Caucasian Sketches" must have been obvious. The man sitting behind me asked if I was a musician … I told him yes, but only if playing the trumpet in the Stanford band 68 years ago counts. It turned out that he played trumpet in the University of Oregon band sixty years ago … And he enjoyed the concert almost as much as I did.

10/15/12

A Liaison Most Foolhardy

FOR HISTORICAL AND CRASS political reasons, the U.S. never stops declaring its affinity for, and dedication to, Israel. Apparently American politicians fear that any animosity toward Israel is political suicide. So, regardless of how Israel abuses, humiliates, or even brutalizes the Palestinians, we pronounce our loyalty and our sponsorship to them, and almost beg them to back off any new territorial confiscation or economic oppression.

Unfortunately this love affair finds the U.S. in the most precarious position in its 236 year history. The reason is simple: our military and economic dominance no longer serves its historic role as a deterrent to a nuclear holocaust. For 67 years our nuclear arsenal operated as a deterrent to WWIII — no SANE opponent would risk nuclear annihilation by our launch-ready missiles. But today's threat is from a new type of enemy, tens of thousands of Muslim jihadists we would not classify as rational, or even sane, because they not only don't fear death — they welcome it as a ticket to martyrdom, especially if it comes in jihad against the American infidels....

It's one thing to fear suicide bombers in Baghdad or Kabul. It's another to fear them as possessors of nuclear weapons and sworn to avenge the hordes of Muslims killed by Americans in Iraq or Afghanistan — or by our well-armed and well-financed partner in Palestine.

There are over a billion Muslims on this planet. They don't all hate Americans, but our senseless destruction of Iraq turned millions of them against us. Our ten year conflict in Afghanistan has obviously turned more against us. And now every Palestinian civilian killed by Israeli bombs and rockets fans the flames of U.S. hatred because even the most illiterate Muslim knows who supplies those Israeli jets and bombs.

It would be comforting if we could control the development and distribution of nuclear weapons in the underdeveloped world, but those days are long gone. So called WMDs (weapons of mass destruction), like the Russian AK47 automatic weapon, are not subject to U.S. arms control, or even democratic nation control. The tiger is out of his cage. Seven or eight countries already have nuclear weapons. How do you foreclose others?

And how do you keep a group of insane and enraged religious fanatics — Muslim jihadists — from using WMD against the American infidels right here in the United States, when they don't fear death themselves, and when we have eight thousand miles of border and no way of intercepting all missiles?

The only hope for a safe future lies in the special talents of the newly-elected U.S. President. Barack Obama at least offers some hope of American-Muslim conciliation because he thinks like a world leader, not an American apologist. He knows that international respect — and American generosity — are probably the only deterrent we have left against fanatical, deranged enemies.

Wish him well. And tell our truculent associate in the Middle East to stop abusing their Palestinian neighbors. They're risking OUR lives, not just theirs.

11/22/12

Part 2

THE TALKING CHINA DOLL

I WAS BEHIND A tiny China doll in the Costco food service line. She was clutching two dollar bills and a large doll. There was no obvious parent ahead of her.

Suddenly she turned and said something to me in a matter-of-fact fashion. I was surprised, then amused, that such a tiny doll could talk, especially to a stranger. I asked her how old she was —"four, or five?" She said "seven," which explained her talking skill, but not her casual gregariousness.

"Are you in second grade?"

"No, first grade" She mentioned something about her doll, thrusting it forward briefly. "What are you going to buy?"

"A berry sundae." Sure enough, the price up there was $1.49, so her two dollar bills were enough.

As we edged forward, she had other bits of casual conversation. Another, older girl in line was equally amused by her verbal spunk and poise. At one point, as she approached the window, she uttered the patented,"

Have a nice day."

I answered in my best Mandarin, "Shay shay."

Finally, as she placed her order, she spoke to a Caucasian man waiting off to the side, for a pizza it turned out. He was amused by my fascination over this tiny talking China doll. I commented on her precociousness and asked him if she spoke any Chinese. He said she knows only a few words — and likes to talk to strangers.

The sad thing is that I'll never see that tiny human again or learn the rest of her undoubtedly amazing life story. And how many other times have I watched, or chatted briefly with, an intriguing or beguiling human being that I would never see again. Never, ever....

2/2/13

Your Psychosocial Score Card:
Libertarians and Tea Partiers in the Quicksand

A M I THE ONLY one who sees a fatal fallacy in the basic tenet of conservatives and libertarians, namely, that the best hope for personal freedom and economic health lies in unhampered capitalism and a minimum of regulation. In today's dialect that translates into a free market economy and limited government.

The Tea Party clan and their right wing Republican colleagues hang their hat on that core mantra. And the massive Federal government is now thoroughly dysfunctional because congress is sufficiently populated with devotees of just such a dialectic.

But the fatal fallacy in that mantra is the assumption that human beings will play by the rules of civilized society, starting with the Golden Rule, out of decency and a sense of fair play. Restraints and regulation are therefore as unnecessary as they are unpleasant. Regimentation is stifling. Taxation is draconian. Government is bureaucracy, which is paralysis.

Who can possibly buy that pipedream in this or any other gathering of homo sapiens? Logical extension of that doctrine would eliminate the necessity of stop signs, speed limits, and penal codes, not to mention tax collectors, police agencies, and armies. Carried to its extreme any free market, free society argument destroys itself.

The fact is that the bedrock assumption of libertarians and dedicated conservatives blandly ignores the darker side of human nature, ancient or modern. It reflects a dangerous naïveté, in fact, because great numbers of the populace will not play straight and fair without restraints and intimidation, in other words without government — and government with teeth. American jails hold almost one per cent of U.S. population, and that number doesn't include millions more of cheats, thieves, exploiters, abusers, and schemers who haven't been caught or haven't yet been covered by appropriate legislation.

Any examination of the freedom vs. regulation question always leads me to what I would call the Morality Corollary, namely, that the degree of regulation required for a given populace is inversely correlated with the moral integrity of that society. The greater the level of immorality, barbarity, inhumanity, or intractability inherent in any society, the greater the requirement for restraint, regulation, governance, and oversight, in short, government, in all its forms. Where conscience, religion, and ethical debate fail, the veneer of civilization requires external restraint and regulation. In other words, Mr. Libertarian, Government.

As you survey the level of morality, ethics, rectitude, and decency in 2013 America, what do you think the chances of smaller government are? Not too good, right? But wouldn't a SMARTER government be lovely?

3/3/13

Vicarious Is Nice,
but not the Real Deal...

WE'VE JUST RETURNED FROM a week on Kauai, my favorite Hawaiian Island. We were host to four generations of the Wills clan, including 7 great grandkids. There was tennis, scuba, snorkeling, and hiking, lots of it. They all had a great time.

So did I, but in a much more muted, sedentary, vicarious fashion than ever before. The reason is, of course, advanced age and its health effects, especially severe osteoarthritis.

Instead of snorkeling the reef, I watched the Poipu surf and lawn frolic from our balcony at Kiahuna. Instead of playing good tennis, I watched good tennis by Generation X and Generation Y, better tennis than I played two and three decades ago on the same courts. Instead of hiking the Na Pali and Kalalau trails, I shopped the stalls at Spouting Horn and the novelty shops in Hanapepe and Kalaheo. Instead of tossing the Frisbee on that huge lawn with our star athletes, I played Sequence with nice ladies on our dining table.

All jaunts were in our big Chrysler to Costco, to Big Save, to Joe's On The Green, to the Waiohai. The exercise was primarily cerebral, reading the papers and doing any crossword in sight.

Maralys and I were the only members of the clan in our Eighties, so were the only ones not in the ocean or on the trails and tennis courts. Twenty five out of twenty seven moving and shaking should make for a pretty good junket. Lots of action and no accidents. What more could we ask for?

Well, maybe a little less arthritis and a lot less weight. And a keener sense of vicarious pleasure in the bleachers while watching the happy warriors cavorting on the field....

3/20/13

God's Angry Warriors

THE U.S. IS SUCH a "law and order" society that its jails and prisons house a number approaching 1 percent of its population, a number exceeding that of any other nation, primitive or developed. And the number of those incarcerated doesn't include hundreds of thousands more who are on parole and thereby one step away from incarceration.

You can ponder all day long why America's prison population leads the world — whether it's religious fervor, a highly-refined judicial system, a surplus of lawyers, or a decaying social structure — but my focus is on the legion of God's angry men and women who persuaded judges and juries to fill — and overfill — our jails and prisons. (Jails are local and usually short term; prisons are State, Federal, and longer term).

I would love to see a psychological profile made of district attorneys and prosecutors in general. How do they differ in personality, motivation, and background from defense attorneys and humans in general? Are they crusaders, angry men and women, vengeful by nature, or simply government-hired attorneys who were handed files to work and informal quotas to meet? Are they merely responding to the challenge of the case, working against that ridiculous "beyond a reasonable doubt" criterion, or are they fueled by some personal grievance or injustice, or by religious or moral indignation?

Obviously not every deputy district attorney handling a heavy load of files at arraignments and preliminary hearings has a personal vendetta, or even a prosecutorial temperament. Many just got there as a decent paying job, something a lot of young attorneys can't find today. And once there, in a criminal calendar courtroom, any good attorney will respond to the challenge of the battle, and the theoretical presumption of innocence imposed by our system of law. But what will he or she do when trying a capital case, or a case with heavy penalties, when some evidence turns up that favors the defense or undercuts the prosecution? Will justice dictate a concession, or will the pressure to convict — to win — prevail? The shows we see on TV, and some of the criminal cases on appeal, reveal gross miscarriages of justice on the part of prosecutors who won by foul means and dirty fighting.

So the question is, were those dirty tactics a product of the pressure inherent in the combat — and the effect on chances of higher office for a prominent prosecutor — or were there character defects involved that may be typical of some prosecutors? Maybe a psychological profile has been done on prosecutors. Are they angry about something in their past? Are they unusually self-righteous? Are they religious activists? Do they get any personal pleasure from sending a defendant to what is really an animal stockade?

If there is a study, cite me to it. If you yourself know what makes prosecutors tick, fill me in. Meanwhile, I intend to stay as far away from them as possible....

4/17/13

DISCRIMINATION TO THE FORE:
A Starring Role

WHEN YOU HAVE GLOBAL interests and a robust curiosity, you are constantly faced with choices, because time is finite. What to read, what to watch on TV, and what to do with your leisure time and discretionary funds.

So it really helps not to be interested in everything that's offered in a supermarket society like the 21st century U.S.

For example, when most food tastes so good that you end up fighting a weight problem, it's almost a pleasure when the vegetable turns out to be squash or Brussels sprouts, and the dessert turns out to be cheesecake or rice pudding. No problem. Thanks for the pass.

And if the TV channel turns into hockey or boxing or soccer, whew, a welcome break, and back to PBS. But if PBS or KCET morphs into modern art or modern dance — emphasis on the "modern" — or into jazz or a cultural bull session, that leaves radio (rarely) or reading (usually). Radio means KUSC, but even classical music can get tedious or boring if it was composed in the last 100 years (Or if it's Schumann, Mahler, or Haydn …)

Rap or jazz or mindless blather pretty much eliminate the non-classical stations, so it's back to the magazines, articles, and annual reports stacked around my chair. The only books nestled there are reference books, the dictionary, and compendia of short historical, scientific, and biographical squibs. The library in the next room, my portion, is full of reference books, texts, and non-fiction discourses. M's section has all of the fairy stories (novels), old and new.…

Mornings go to the newspapers and the stock market (CNBC) unless there's a major disaster on TV (WWIII or equivalent). All other daytime TV causes more brain damage than the NFL and IED concussions.…

The afternoons go to crosswords, paper work (like taxes and bills), chores, watering the plantation, and errands (shopping, P.O., bank). Then the evenings go to the mail and TV — news, Jeopardy, NOVA, Frontline, Moyer, and British shows like New Tricks, Doc Martin, and Death in Paradise. Not to mention six series of symphony, musicals, and plays (season tickets).

Three or four trips a year fill out the calendar. One seems to be a cruise and another a trip to Hawaii or the Caribbean. It sounds like a posh life, but I think the infirmities of old age make us deserve it. And switching from combat as a mercenary soldier for insurance companies to playing in the world's biggest gambling casino (NYSE and NASDAQ) has made it all affordable — that and never paying a penny of interest on anything, ever, for 40 years … A depression mentality has paid off, that and some thoughtful scanning of stocks for those 40 years.

All of which I call a multifarious but discriminating life. Who said that discrimination is bad? Without it, you'd be a leaf blowing in the wind. Let's hear it for benign, therapeutic discrimination that lets you focus on what you enjoy and what you're good at.

5/7/13

PLEASE MR. MAILMAN:
Don't Turn Into A Corporate Cadet...

The USPS has served the U.S. well for over a century and is the primary link between millions of rural Americans and the outside world. It's the only inexpensive non-electronic means of transmitting documents and parcels to far flung locations. Aside from the Internet it's the only way to move an ounce of documents thousands of miles for 46 cents. And usually in no more than two days.

But this ancient and widely-respected institution is in serious jeopardy today, undercut by deadly competition and under attack by dedicated political enemies. The competition for first class mail – letters and messages and documents — is lethal because it is the cost-free, instantaneous Internet, which provides "no contest" competition from homes and offices having Internet electronics. This includes the vast majority of businesses and a majority of residences. Email has decimated first class mail, making small, serial postage rate increases a futile response. The dwindling number of isolated, non-electronic households sending letters and documents by mail cannot support the current mammoth postal service organization.

Which leads us to the overwhelming majority of today's mail volume, commonly referred to as junk mail. The rates for second and third class mail, and bulk mailings, are artificially low and contribute grossly to the increasing USPS deficits. What the strident critics of the USPS deficits fail to acknowledge, or maybe even fail to know, is that the ridiculously low rates for junk mail were set by the same devotees of a "free market" that are calling for the privatization of the USPS today. The USPS has to rely on the Postal Regulatory Commission, a panel of political appointees who have to work with a body representing the mail order business in setting postal rates. Relying on political appointees to save the USPS bottom line is like relying on foxes to protect the hen house....

I think there's an irony in the works. The same "free market" stalwarts in the Republican congress who want the USPS privatized obviously haven't thought about what privatization will do to the postage rates charged for junk mail by a for-profit organization like Fed Ex or UPS. The venture capitalists or wealthy investors who organize Fraud Ex aren't going to make the political angels of Free Market congressmen very happy when they eliminate the outrageous subsidy for junk mail and charge the real cost of delivering mountains of junk mail to millions of mail boxes....

Oh yes, it will almost be laughable if the USPS assassins lose their Chamber of Commerce angels when Fraud Ex operates at a profit. First class mail would be priced out of existence and junk mailers would be screaming like eagles at the realistic rates.

Fans of Ronald Reagan and Margaret Thatcher would relish the privatization of the USPS — and probably many other governmental bodies. But anyone who rode the British trains before Thatcher privatized them would be disappointed by British Rail today, as we were. And anyone who remembers when America had a true middle class partly fueled by labor unions can thank Ronnie and his devotees for what is becoming a two-class society.

If USPS is to survive, it certainly needs remedial action. Postal rates for all classes must be raised. When you compare Fed Ex and UPS rates, current first class rates are almost as ridiculously low as bulk mail rates. Saturday delivery is an unnecessary luxury. Routes can be reorganized. And the pension plan, like most pension plans created by politicians rather than actuaries, is apparently bloated and underfunded. Like so many out-of-control or underfunded governmental pension plans in the country, there are probably only 3 solutions — renegotiation, default, or bankruptcy ... I doubt that a government agency can go bankrupt as such (as Orange County did), and congress might not tolerate default. But the pension plan of new employees could probably be redesigned in today's tough job market, and the plan for existing employees might be vulnerable to some adjustments or cash payout offers.

In any case, I, for one, hope that USPS management and congress can salvage a sound old ship that's taking on water. It would be a shame to have a corporate cadet delivering mail three times a week at triple the cost, with different rates for "regular," "priority," and "overnight." The only consolation would be to invest in Fraud Ex stock and share a little of the venture capitalists' profits....

5/13/13

Does "Homeless" Make You Cringe?

How do you feel when you come face to face with a panhandler or a vagrant carrying a "Homeless" sign? Or see a story about the problems of children attending school while living in a car?

I know how I feel. It's a combination of discomfort and sympathy. The discomfort comes from the gross disparity of our positions, a raw sort of injustice, a primal instinct that I should do something.

The sympathy reminds me that I still have a streak of humanity in me, to feel vicarious pain from another human's obvious misery. Then, too, there's a twinge if I don't roll down the car window and tender a $5 or $10 bill I would never miss.

For whatever reason, I don't get a sense of "there but for the grace of God go I." But I do know that the wretch out there, while not my son or daughter, is someone's son or daughter, or maybe someone's parent....

Ronald Reagan fans would be quick to remind me that most or all of the homeless got there through stupidity or addiction, but that claim doesn't absolve the pangs of sympathy a comfortable human being should feel on seeing another human in obviously miserable condition, with almost no hope of resolution.

Whether the derelict is an addict, an alcoholic, or a criminal doesn't alter the fact that the dingy, disheveled person standing or sitting there is miserable to the core, way beyond embarrassed or depressed. The pain is there, regardless of the cause, and no addict or scoundrel gets too low to experience the humiliation over being an outcast in an affluent society. Every derelict had parents and may have siblings. Maybe even children. But, for whatever reason, they have no one to turn to in their misery. And too often even the Salvation Army and other shelters are overbooked, overburdened, or unavailable for more than a few days.

The days of the happy hobo, riding with pals on freight trains, and living under bridges or in hobo camps, are over. There are now so many homeless derelicts and outcasts that they are a major urban problem and the subject of increasing laws and ordinances designed to make them go away, to somewhere else. Anywhere else....

No government today has a solution for the new wave of poverty and homelessness. No federal, state, or local solution is in place. There are "refugee" camps all over the globe, to take in hundreds of thousands displaced by war and revolution. But not in the U.S.

So all the politicians can do is adopt ordinances and instruct the police to keep the homeless and the destitute moving, out of sight if possible. They are now in effect a waste product of an industrialized and gentrified society, something to sideline and dispose of as practically as possible. It's not a question of emotions or empathy. It's a question of political reality — economics and law and order....

It's when I see them that I get uncomfortable. I know I can't help them for more than an instant, if at all. But when one looks at me and pleads for something, I am shaken inside. And I know that in a decent, humane society, even a homeless wretch would have somewhere to go to eat and sleep. A mercy mission with some sort of a rehab attempt. You would think that the richest nation on earth could afford some sort of last resort refuge for human wreckage.

But it doesn't. So all you can do is feel sorry for the human driftwood somewhere out there in the night. And think about much more pleasant things in our comfy surroundings....

6/7/13

THE CREEPING ISOLATION OF
A SURVIVOR

ONLY A FEW WHO read this will know what I'm
talking about. Because the reality of the process
doesn't sink in until the late '80s or '90s in a world
where humans live ten years longer than they used to.

Forty years ago a seventy year old would start to
notice that his classmates and childhood friends had
quietly departed this world, and he was attending more
and more funerals. And, to add to his sense of isolation,
he would have noticed that lifestyles and social mores
were in a state of flux, leaving behind the attitudes and
social structures he knew in the post WWII years when
he got set in the world.

Vietnam and the drug culture of the Seventies
fractured Yankee America's middle class values, and
then the Silicon Valley revolution altered the landscape
even more, to the point where Generation X got married to the computer and Generation Y has almost left
traditional society completely, in a never-ending stream
of e mails, texts, and twitters.

So those of us born 85 or more years ago find the landscape almost completely void of our childhood friends, high school and college classmates, parents, most husbands of close friends, and serious, unhurried discussion with family and friends. Contemporary friends are dead or disabled, particularly the males. Our Baby Boomer children are now middle-aged and busier than ever, with full agendas and tenuous retirement prospects.

Their kids, our Generation X grandkids, are coping with increasing economic challenges in the new Millennium and following social, recreational, and athletic schedules that keep them on the run – with less and less leisure time and glued to their little electronic partners.

Our Generation Y great grandkids are programmed almost 24 hours a day, cell phone and Iphone bound, and destined never to know the joys of a fishing hole, a swimming hole, or blueberry picking, or unsupervised play in the woods.

I would never trade my totally unsupervised childhood in the Vermont woods or on Florida beaches for the regimented rat-race I see Generation X and Generation Y running. Actually, I feel silently sorry about the frenetic, stress-wracked world that we are leaving them after the technological and ideological evolution of the Twentieth Century....

But my point here is that most friends and

acquaintances have departed my world, and the social and intellectual landscape I see around me has grown more and more foreign to my tastes and interests.

Not to worry though. Despite my growing sense of isolation and abandonment as a "sole survivor," there is still enough social and intellectual activity in my life to satisfy my needs, I still have enough fitness to get around without assistance, and we still control enough capital to live comfortably for the indefinite future, and even to share some bounty with the next three generations....

7/20/13

A Thousand Cries For Help

I KNEW THAT SYRIA, Iraq, and Afghanistan are a mess, with Egypt and Libya close behind. But I didn't know that the entire world, including the U.S., is teetering on the edge of disaster, medically, environmentally, and economically.

That is, until I finally dumped a huge box of mail onto a patio table and went through it yesterday. The mail had accumulated at the P.O. while we were on our August UK-Norway-Ireland cruise, and last week I pulled out the pieces that looked important. But that left a couple of hundred envelopes, large and small, that looked like they could wait a few days.

How could I be so cruel? Thousands of colts are being slaughtered so that Pfizer can make Premarin for ladies. Wild horses are being sold by BLM to buyers for pet food factories. Hundreds of rescued big cats are running out of food in Texas, Oregon, Tennessee, and Ohio — and the older ones need expensive vet care. Dogs and cats, even horses, pigs, and goats, are being left to starve by foreclosed owners. Crippled donkeys and burros are slated for execution. Draft horses aren't properly retired to pasture. Big cats are being raised in Texas specifically for operators of U.S. "safari" hunts on private ranches.

But that's just the animals. Native populations in Sub-Saharan Africa and Southeast Asia are starving, malnourished, ravished by malaria, AIDS, river blindness, and birth defects. Andean and Amazonian natives need help. The hospital ship Mercy performs surgery on thousands of West Africans. The Smile Train finances hundreds of surgeries on facial and oral deformities. The City of Hope and St. Jude need money. So does Sloan-Kettering. So do something like thirty foundations and societies focusing on American disease and disability, five for the eye alone.

And, of course, the environment is being brutalized by mining companies, energy companies, coal-fired power plants, industrial waste, fossil fuels, nuclear spills, and even bovine flatulence. The Sierra Club, Environmental Defense Fund, WWF, Wildlife Federation, Rainforest Alliance, Nature Conservancy, Greenpeace, and Earthjustice are just a few of the firms reminding us that we are trashing the planet for our grandchildren (in our case, our ten great grandchildren...).

Not to mention the political and economic funeral notices, three or four daily. Both parties are desperate and running out of dire warnings that the enemy is getting stronger and more dangerous. The Democrats are worried and frustrated. The Republicans are paranoid. I read almost none of it. It's a torrent of desperation and I can't cure a dysfunctional government with my checkbook.

But the Quakers have a signal point: the DOD military budget takes up 57 percent of the U.S. budget. That's $1.2 million dollars for each minute of the year. If you really want to profile the U.S. persona, that 57 percent for "military" compares with 6 percent for education and 5 percent for health...

But perhaps the most heart-rending appeal I opened was about saving FIFI as a natural treasure. You see FIFI — lovely photos — is the one and only remaining B-29 bomber that can still fly (and maybe drop another atomic bomb...). How can we let such a glorious symbol of American success in WWII become extinct? She needs work after 68 years. Please send a check....

I won't be sending any checks this week, not with a sizable five figures due for estimated income tax in ten days. But we do support the population and environmental organizations in December, not to mention several groups fighting to keep religion out of government. Planned Parenthood, Earthjustice, and Population Connection (formerly ZPG) to name some of the good ones. I'm a big cat guy (reincarnation, no doubt), so I do support WWF and a couple of the big cat guardians. But I am now so cynical politically that Maralys is the only hope for the "firewall" appeals to combat organized red state ignorance (otherwise known as the Tea Party)....

Yesterday brought a whole new batch of cries for help. If our mail and the Internet are any example, one of America's growth industries is the multitude of SOS organizations pleading for help through our mailbox, our computer, and our telephone.

9/4/13

WATER, WATER EVERYWHERE:
Lifeguard Ahoy

T HE ENGLISH-SPEAKING WORLD SEEMS to like triads. It started early, with The Father, The Son, and The Holy Ghost, then Faith, Hope, and Charity. Next came Life, Liberty, and The Pursuit of Happiness, Bell, Book, and Candle, Page, Chapter, and Verse, Lock, Stock, and Barrel, Tall, Dark, and Handsome, and Ready, Willing, and Able.

Who hasn't heard of Hart, Shaffner, and Marx, or Peter, Paul, and Mary? Then there are lots of triad law firms, like Gibson, Dunn, and Crutcher, Bonne, Jones, and Bridges, Rose, Klein, and Marias.

In the Forties a peppy blonde named Betty Hutton sang an equally peppy song called Doctor, Lawyer, and Indian Chief. Now, seven decades later, the triad would probably be Doctor, Lawyer, and Financial Planner, the 3 people who probably have the most influence on your long term welfare. Unless your house is on fire, or you desperately need a zoning variance, or you are being assaulted and robbed, a fireman, a politician, or a policeman is not going to have a vital influence on your future well-being. But the doctor, lawyer, and financial planner all have great potential for actually shaping your future, especially your long term future.

The technician who comes closest to determining whether you even have a future, or what it will be like, is obviously the doctor. He has the potential for determining life or death, good health or ill health, full function or partial function. He or she may not keep you alive forever, or even well for long, but no one else can come close to the role medicine will play in your life, especially the later stages.

This seems crystal clear to me in this special environment we're in at the moment. The M.S. Nautica has about 684 passengers on board as we cruise up The North Sea, and the average age of the multitude looks to be well above sixty. As we survey the semi-affluent crowd, it seems obvious that lawyers and financial planners played a role in getting a lot of them here, because cruises cost money. And money is what lawyers and financial planners are expected to gather for future cruisers, in one way or another.

But the last technician some of the codgers and their wives probably saw before the cruise, and the first crew member they want to see if there is a problem on board, is the nurse, then the doctor, without whom the ship could never have left Southampton. No one would ask if there's a lawyer or a financial planner on staff and on board. We can deal with them later, and at arm's length. But who would sail for more than a day with no doctor and nurse on board, in the token clinic down on deck 4? That fact alone tells you what is critical professional care for the aged or the infirm, and what isn't.

Already, on our third day out, a Royal Navy helicopter has come to the Nautica and transported an ailing crew member to a hospital in Hull, England. Whether that young crew member lives or dies will depend on medical care. Whether any aged passenger who suffers a myocardial infarction in the next 9 days lives or dies will depend entirely on the availability and competency of one or more doctors.

But whether a passenger suffers a steep Dow Jones loss, or learns during the cruise that he or she has been sued at home, is no match for the medical risk in transit, or the medical outcome if treatment is necessary. So I rest my case on the issue of who is the pivotal professional for any passenger on this ship in August, 2013.

But all a cruise does is highlight a fact of life, an inalienable reality. We are born as a medical event. Our death will be a medical event. And an ongoing primary concern as we pass through life, long or short, is the availability — and competency — of medical care, specifically the work of doctors.

So forget any debate over who is the premium

profession among all the premium professions. A cruise is simply the easiest way to answer the question. The chips are down in a full-service microcosm surrounded by an endless expanse of cold sea water.

8/17/3

Is it the Heat or the Humidity?

Have you ever noticed that almost all of the poverty-stricken and afflicted populations of planet Earth fall within a geographic band known as The Torrid Zone, or, more familiarly, The Tropics? Take a look at the globe one of these days and note where the Tropic of Cancer and Tropic of Capricorn circle the globe. An answer to a trivia question is that the two Tropic parallels lie 23 degrees and 26 minutes above and below the Equator, or approximately 26 percent of the distance from the Equator to the Poles. The area between the Tropic parallels is what we call the Torrid Zone or The Tropics, and it obviously makes up 26 percent of the geographic arc between the Poles.

The Tropics are noteworthy for disparate features, both related to temperature and humidity. The first thing I think of when the "tropics" are mentioned is the hundreds of sites we usually regard as forms of tropical paradise, with warm blue-green sea, blue sky, waving palms, balmy (humid) breezes, and a torpid, leisurely pace supported by comfy amenities. Clothing is loose and casual — or optional. The stress of work, home, and family is thousands of miles away. The indigenous population is either serving your needs or just out of sight. Unless you are allergic to heat and humidity, it's nice while it lasts.

But that same heat and humidity have had a different historical effect on the native populations in The Torrid Zone. Although the Tropics may have been the cradle of human evolution, assuming that Central Africa was the spawning ground of homo erectus and homo sapiens, take a look at where modern civilization developed —and where it didn't develop.

Run your finger through the Tropics in South and Central America, mid-continent Africa, and Southeast Asia, then ask yourself what percentage of the earth's poorest and least developed populations fall squarely in that band. I don't know what the academic studies on meteorology and nation building have shown, but it's clear enough that the bulk of international relief and philanthropy aimed at underdeveloped countries ends up in the Torrid Zone, not the Temperate Zones like the U.S., Canada, Northern Europe, Argentina, South Africa, and Australia.

I'm sure I'm not the first to claim that the same torpor and lassitude we seek in our posh tropical paradise has been the obstacle to empire building by the indigenous populations of those idylls. There is apparently no etymologic link between the words "tropic" and "torpor," but there probably should be. Heat and humidity cause torpor, if not stupor, in denizens of the Temperate Zone —ask Maralys about the last 10 days here over 90 degrees (even our cats went catatonic) — and they must take something off the edge of industry in the native populations.

If not, why is it that the missionaries, crusaders of every stripe, and welfare stalwarts (think CARE, Unicef, Peace Corps) head for underdeveloped populations in Central Africa, Southern India, Indonesia, Southern Mexico, and Central America? Why are the major cities all in the Temperate Zones?

I submit to you that the industrial depression in the hot zone isn't merely a product of human torpor. There's another form of life that LOVES heat and humidity, and thrives on it. It's a form you can't see, without a microscope. I'm referring to pathogens of every type, bacteria, viruses, and fungi — not to mention the creepy crawlers you can see. The Tropics may be a relaxing sauna or steam room to a New York industrialist on vacation. But to a virus or a bacterium or a fungus, the heat and humidity are a delightful Petri dish in which to incubate. So the humans down South are on Valium while the pathogens are on steroids…

Why are Tropical Diseases and Parasitology increasingly important medical subjects in a peripatetic world? Because tropical populations have had to endure some ravages we don't encounter in the Temperate

Zone, scourges that undoubtedly contributed to industrial retardation in the Hot Zone.

So as the humans wilt, the pathogens party. The little bugs may help to explain why tourist resorts are the growth industry in the tropics, not industrial empire building.

In the meanwhile, Maralys is so intolerant of heat and humidity that we have a new heating and A/C system being installed next week. And it will continue to be hard to get my Type A Temperate Zone wife back to my favorite tropical resorts.

9/12/13

It Really *Is* A Small World...

MOST PEOPLE HAVE AT least one "small world" experience. It's either a "fancy meeting you here" encounter or the discovery of an object or activity in a most unexpected place. It's a form of eerie experience with something totally unexpected or totally out of place. It's an unlikely, uncanny coincidence.

We've probably had more than our share because we have traveled extensively and lived a long time doing it. I'm going to record three of them for the record so that we don't forget the details in the fog of time. They all involve travel, in each case to a spot far from home, which helps to define a "small world" encounter. Two involve a most unlikely encounter, one that defied all odds. The third involved a laugh, followed by a close-to-home coincidence.

The first was a stunner. In 1975 we took Tracy and Kirk, our two youngest, to Europe for one of our unstructured adventures. We had been on similar excursions with the older kids before, but never on the Orient Express out of Paris. I'm not sure how far we intended to go on the way to Istanbul, but the trip was a nightmare that first night, scary and grotesque.

We got locked off in first class, with the kids trapped several cars behind, surrounded by a scary troop of peasants — and their animals. No one had beds and no one spoke English, or admitted to it. I was threatening to open the locked train car door with a fire axe when the train stopped in the middle of nowhere, in the middle of the night. Doors suddenly unlocked, Maralys jumped off the train and ran back to where she thought the kids might be, then jumped back on. I joined them in their exotic menagerie and we finished a harrowing night.

As you can imagine, the 4 of us de-trained in the early A.M. and found ourselves in Montreaux, Switzerland, which may as well have been Timbuktu. For whatever reason, we took a tram railway up a nearby mountain to a small Alpine town called Leysin, where, we later learned, Americans come to attend university classes and ski....

We remember only 3 things about Leysin, Switzerland . The first is that all the Alpine cows wore collars with bells hanging from them, so their movement was musical. The second is that we knew enough French to know what "pique-nique interdit" meant in the park (picnics prohibited). And the third memory is our first "small world" experience.

In walking around that Alpine village, we came

on the ski gondola station and sporthaus. I looked in the window of a sports shop there and couldn't believe my eyes. The poster on display was a familiar shot of Chris Wills flying a hang glider into the sun at Torrey Pines, California — about seven-thousand miles away from Leysin and about two years earlier. The same photo had been used by Hang Ten on school notebooks — without our consent — so they sent us a box of the notebooks....

Chris had been the first U.S. hang gliding champion in October, 1973, then was runner-up to Bobby the next year. Only weeks before our unexpected visit to Leysin, Bobby and Chris had finished filming the Twentieth Century Fox movie "Skyriders" in Greece, then Bobby had won the British Hang Gliding championship at Mere, Wiltshire, with the four of us present.

The second small world shock came four years ago in a small village in Central Vermont. The odds of it happening were again nil. In scanning the Wall Street Journal in my family room chair one day I noticed a Rutland, Vermont dateline — I lived there at age twelve — so I scanned the front page article. It was about a couple who had hiked the Appalachian Trail all the way up from Georgia and pulled off long enough to earn some money as casual labor in the Rutland area. I thought no more of it.

A few weeks later, six of us took a ten day cruise on our old pal, the Crystal Symphony, from Boston to

Montreal. After disembarking in Montreal, we headed for Boston through Vermont, my old stomping ground. After a night in Stowe, we headed south for a country inn we like in Landgrove, near Weston. We stopped for lunch at a country store in Pittsfield and got into a discussion with the owner. Then, for some reason I can't recall, we visited his converted barn at his nearby farm.

I had a ruptured patellar tendon since our stop in Halifax, Nova Scotia, so waited outside the barn while the other 5 climbed up and down stairs in the building. I'm no casual chatterer, but I did have a brief conversation with a fit-looking young woman who was about to leave on a bicycle. When she said she was just temporary labor, I asked from where. When she said she had been hiking the Appalachian Trail, I said, Please tell me you don't have a hiking partner…She said she did, and he was also working on the same farm … Please tell me you weren't recently written up in the WSJ … She was. They were the couple I had read about two weeks before and three-thousand miles away.

My group and the farm owner were as flabbergasted as I was at the freaky coincidence. Even the employer hadn't known that the couple had been written up as a feature story in the world's leading financial newspaper.

The third event was almost comical, and just 23 days ago. Our last stop, the ninth, on our UK-Norway-Ireland cruise in August, was at Portland, in Southwest

England, an important naval base during WWII. Maralys and I went on an excursion to Corfe Castle, about 20 miles north of the seaside resort of Weymouth. We got a good view of the Dorset countryside from a front seat of the "coach" (bus, here), then had a half mile hike around the base of the formidable castle and castle town, high on a hill.

At one point the group stopped while the guide was obviously pointing out part of the castle up the hill. Those of us in the rear, unable to hear, simply stood and waited, seeing nothing under the trees. Soon a plaintive, slightly petulant female voice behind us asked, "What are we looking at?" We all started laughing, and did so more in the coach on the way back.

As it turned out, the questioner sat behind us. As we celebrated her pique, the usual questions arose. Where are you from? We said California, an area called Orange County. She laughed and said that she and her husband live in Morningside, in Fullerton, California. We told her that Maralys had spoken there — she does the old folks beautifully — and we get lots of invitations for a free lunch there....

Small world again. Especially since we had met no other Orange County denizens among the 684 M.S. Nautica passengers during a twelve day cruise....

9/18/13

91

Sorry, GOP — Your "America" Isn't Coming Back....

E VEN THOUGH WE RIDICULE about 90 percent of the GOP agenda around here, I think I understand the emotional mindset behind it. When they rail about "taking back" America, I know exactly what they mean. And I also know that their goal is getting farther away every year that goes by.

The Republicans want the America that I grew up in, just before WWII. It was white and it was Boy Scouts and it was *Dr. Kildare* and *Father Knows Best*, and it was church on Sunday. Mexicans didn't do the housework and the yard work. Blacks didn't dominate football and basketball. Chinese weren't buying up estates and foreclosures. Vietnamese weren't running the nail salons. Doctors didn't have Indian and Arab names. "Welfare" was rare and out of sight. People worked for one employer, saved for retirement, and retired at 65.

There were no food stamps or IRA's or 401K's. There were no Walmarts or Targets or Costcos, just merchants, shopkeepers, and the Sears catalogue.

There was no OSHA or EPA, no class actions, no flood of claims-hungry attorneys. And unemployment relief was brief, if available at all.

So by "bring back America" Republicans mean, but aren't saying, bring back the simple, white, homogeneous America I knew in a New England town in 1940, where homosexuality, abortion, prostitution, illegitimacy, pornography, and infidelity were out of sight and out of mind.

The other plank in the GOP platform boils down to "get the government out of our lives and, while you're at it, get God back in our lives." Having grown up in a staunch Republican family, I'm thoroughly versed in that creed. Although they say that Ronald Reagan would be shocked by the anti-government creed of the Tea Party Republican wing today, he did inspire the mantra that "government is the problem, not the solution," and there is no question that the arm of government — federal, state, and local — now reaches far deeper into our lives than it did seventy five years ago in Yankee USA.

Dealing with some governmental bureaucracies can inspire a Tea Party emotion, and a lot of American politicians are a disgrace on display. But white Yankee America isn't coming back and neither is a governmental retreat from D.C. to the village square. The Tea Party may stultify Washington, D.C. for a short while, but it won't shrink or overhaul government in the long run.

No, sorry Republicans, your upset and disappointment with brown, chaotic, regulated America is understandable. But your hopes and goals are fruitless and your obstructionist platform is destructive, instead of constructive. Anachronism is not going to lead to progress or solutions. It COULD lead to a shrinking minority party....

Your siren call is to a shrinking white middle-aged male constituency. Better revamp and reorient. Study the new demographics. And work on an agenda designed to make them the best they can be. Or get out of the way and let the Democrats run the show.

11/16/13

Part 3

RIDE OUT THE STORM:
IT's PROBABLY SMARTER.

WHEN YOU HAVE A 65th wedding anniversary, people tend to ask you to spell out the secrets of such a long marriage. My original reaction was to pass it off as pleasantry, but then I decided to define the factors that made such a long union possible.

In the last analysis, longevity in our case probably boils down to a few unique factors and a few generic elements. Husbands and wives usually cite different features of a prolonged marriage; in fact, male and female brains see almost any question from a slightly different angle. But Maralys agrees with most of the attributes I cite for our longevity, and would, of course, add a few of her own.

Here are the elements I cite for the longevity of a marriage that would have defied the predictions of most acquaintances in 1949…

We both had a lot of energy. Both physical and intellectual energy. Anyone who knew us at Stanford and San Jose would have cited a high level of "life force" or vitality in us. We were smart — despite my D in Organic Chemistry after we met — and we had plenty of opinions we were happy to share. Not oppressive, just lively....

Even aside from the sex thing, we started out as friends. And, looking back, we both agree that spouses have to start as friends and stay friends for the long haul.

Then there was the attitude about marriage. I came from a time when marriage was the gold standard, not a trial partnership, and a time when couples rode out the usual midlife crises by staying together "for the children" (in my parents' case, for "the child"). Couples in the pre-WWII era seem to have had a clearer vision of the devastating effect of divorce on children than those who grew out of the Beat and Yuppie and Me generations in the late twentieth century, when divorce became option #1.

I appreciate the fact that my parents stayed together, even though both had traditional "grounds" for divorce, and it was obvious to both of them in their seventies, eighties, and nineties(!) that they made the right decision. Those are years when it's no fun — and not even safe — to live alone, or to descend on an offspring's family.

Actually, the need for a partner to share the rigors and frustrations of old age is one very large reason couples should be very slow to divorce during those almost-inevitable midlife crises. It's one thing to have grounds for divorce, most often involving the opposite sex, and it's another to venture out into that no-man's land of divorcées, widows and widowers, and chronic singles. What the midlife divorcées don't realize is how important the team approach becomes as the partners age.

In our experience, even the liveliest and the fittest need a partner in the end. I never would have imagined how important a partner would become in my 80s (and 90s) when it comes to managing a large family, sizable trips, and the never-ending maintenance problems of home, body, and finances....

Which is why I'm glad that Maralys was wise enough, and dedicated enough, to persevere when I gave her "grounds" thirty or forty years ago. She decided I was a good enough package to ride out the problem and let sanity prevail. She's glad, too, because we're as strong a team today as we were in 1949. And that's saying a lot.

Oh, and by the way, I've decided to forgive or live with all of Maralys' irritating, frustrating peccadilloes....

1/5/14

How About Some Noblesse Oblige in California?

T HE CONCEPT OF NOBLESSE oblige — nobility has obligations — seems to be moribund, if not dead, in affluent, laissez-faire, free market America. The rich get richer and the poor stay poor. In fact, the mood on the right side of the aisle in congress is to stop mollycoddling the indolent and unproductive segment of the population with extended unemployment benefits, food stamps, Head Start, and other safety net programs that cost money.

When you think of it, the concept of noblesse oblige is in direct conflict with traditional American "rugged individualism," not to mention the jungle doctrines of Ayn Rand followers and Tea Party Patriots.

Well, if there's any room for noblesse oblige in Horatio Alger America, there's one group that could do a lot of social and economic good by applying a wealth of unexploited talent. And it's a program I haven't yet heard proposed, officially or otherwise. And if it's needed anywhere in the world, I think California would be number one, for several reasons.

I'll cite the reasons and then, hopefully, you'll see the program as a natural. California has a huge population, larger than great numbers of nations at 38 million. California also has a larger than average number of retirees because of its famous climate and geographic and recreational diversity. So California must have a retired population somewhere north of five million. Oodles of them are retired military men and women.

Turn next to another area where California leads the nation in numbers and the world in rates. That's the prison population, recently clocked at 158,000 in 33 state prisons (not including county jails, which now house hundreds of relocated state prisoners).

The California prison system is a horrendous mess, both economic and humanitarian, to the point where Federal judges have ordered changes and the CA Dept. of Corrections is shipping out thousands of prisoners to three other states (Arizona, Mississippi, and Oklahoma) which collect rent for them (to pay Correction Corp. of America and other for-profit prison systems)....

What the statistics don't show, and isn't generally known, is that CA prisons abandoned any effort at rehabilitation years ago and focus simply on confinement at most of the 33 prisons. Confinement consists of exactly that, and in extremely congested conditions, with occupancy at 150 percent or more of specified building design capacity. There are no libraries, class-rooms, computers, or telephones. There is no job train-ing or education as such. There is just TV and a little exercise, but mostly dead time — for years.

Anything a prisoner didn't know about crime when he entered prison he is apt to learn while there. The only schooling is by "guardhouse lawyers" and hard core crooks. Most of what they learn from a prison population only adds to the risk of recidivism, where CA is a leader at approximately 50 percent. Nothing they learn prepares them for a job or useful activity when they get out. (And finding a job is hard for even a competent, trained ex-con.)

I think you can see where I'm heading. For every prisoner simply doing time for years, at a cost of $20,000 plus paid by CA taxpayers, there must be at least one retired engineer, policeman, doctor, military officer, or teacher who has a little spare time and who lives within 50 miles of one of the 33 CA state pris-ons. It wouldn't take any teaching skill or experience to mentor a few interested inmates or to conduct an informal class in the retiree's field. Anyone who teaches or gives speeches knows that having to speak on a sub-ject can be as rewarding for the speaker as the student. And how many retirees need a little challenge after a bygone career?

There's a Pasadena program called Friends Outside, offering solace and support to abandoned families of prisoners. What I'm proposing might be called Friends Inside. I don't know what the details would be — I'm not an administrator — but I do know from first hand experience how much retired talent is not always on a cruise or in the garden. And I know how dismal and vacant the daily schedule is for violators who are rotting away on the inside, but due out into society someday.

1/15/14

THE ULTIMATE GAMBLING CASINO:
The Jury Box

HOW OFTEN HAVE YOU heard people react to reported jury verdicts with "How could they do that?" or "What's the matter with that jury?." The O.J. Simpson, Stand Your Ground (Zimmerman), and Fullerton Police beating (Kelly Thomas) verdicts were just the most notorious examples of popular disgust with jury verdicts.

But bitterness and shock after a jury verdict are everyday events in the thousands of courtrooms in the U.S. Although most litigation is resolved through settlements, plea bargains, arbitration, and court decisions, there are hundreds of criminal and civil jury verdicts rendered every week, and the angry losers retreat in silent bitterness (or philosophical resolve — "Oh well, we gave it a shot")… Only a tiny percentage of high profile litigants or outrageous cases attract the press. The rest of the verdict losers walk away deciding that they had a dumb jury, a weak attorney, or an unfair judge. A few appeal to a higher court, with only a 10–25 percent chance of a reversal.

Only rarely are jurors in a high profile case inter-
viewed publicly after a surprising verdict. The attorneys
trying the case are usually free to question jurors after
the case is terminated and the jurors are excused, but
most jurors exit the courtroom rapidly and can't wait
to escape the courthouse. Trials move too slowly and
laboriously for most jurors — lots of duplication and
repetition — and many of them, after days and days
of trial, are sick of the attorneys on both sides. In my
experience over 25 years of cases, we had to be lucky to
catch up with a juror leaving the courtroom, and even
luckier to have one comment on their deliberations and
reasoning. I don't know how many trial lawyers today
have associates waiting to catch and interview jurors
as they flee the courthouse, especially after a long and
hard-fought trial.

Trial firms spend more time and money on the
front end of a jury trial. Some law firms even "try"
high end cases informally before a mock jury to try to
anticipate jury emotions. Then they retain psychology
"experts"(LOL) to help them select and eliminate prospective jurors during voir dire. Any experienced trial
lawyer knows that a case may be won or lost at the
outset, depending on the luck of the draw in seating,
and excusing, the prospective jurors.

Every juror sitting in the box brings with him or
her bias, opinions, prejudice, and sympathies developed

over decades of life experience. In the limited time allowed for voir dire in modern courtrooms, it's absolutely impossible to divine those prejudices and attitudes. And it's impossible to predict what personality clashes may develop in the jury room over days or weeks of confined contact. All the trial attorneys can do is to try to excuse jurors with abrasive or eccentric personalities, or with life experience, such as education and jobs, that might tilt the juror in one direction or another. In my opinion, doing that is about a third of the trial lawyer's job in trying a jury case.

Only occasionally do we hear from a juror what went on in the jury room, and in his or her mind in rendering a verdict. There isn't a lot of lay literature on jury emotions and deliberations. I would hope that law schools in 2014 pay much more attention to jury selection and jury deliberation than we got at UCLA Law School in 1953. We did have eminent Los Angeles judges come to conduct a mock court trial, but no jury selection training.

I haven't tried a jury case in 15 years, so I'm out of touch. But in view of the little change I saw in 45 years of practice, I suspect that picking a jury today is as much a game of chance as it was 15 years ago. You still have to rely on the luck of the draw (the jury panel sent up), your limited personal questioning during voir dire, and your best hunches and intuition. And there's even a limit on that; you get only a few peremptory challenges (excuse without giving a reason) and the rules on challenges for cause get stricter and stricter as judges try to move trials along.

To say that trying a case to a jury is a crapshoot is no exaggeration. I won cases I should have lost, and lost a couple I should have won. But the difference between a crap game and a jury trial is huge. The odds in a crap game, or in twenty one, or in roulette, are calculable, if not posted. In a courtroom the odds are completely in the laps of the gods. They aren't calculable and they aren't posted. And the best attorney doesn't always win.

2/6/14

The Incredible Shrinking Literati; The Slow Decline of the Planet's Premier Tongue.

MAYBE I'M A COMMITTEE of one, but I think we should be worried about the slow death of the literary portion of the English language. English ranks as the richest and most voluminous language on the planet, both because it incorporated so many words from the other tongues and because the English speaking world became dominant in education and literature since Gutenberg and the Dark Ages.

Estimates of the English vocabulary range in six figures, but it's a dynamic figure because of technological and cultural additions since the Industrial Revolution and subtractions through disuse and Populist aversion to "fancy" language. The Oxford English Dictionary is probably the gold standard for the English tongue, but it requires constant revision for new technological and coined words and acronyms, or for words gone archaic through disuse or cultural shift (cf. "gay").

But I see a seismic shift in the vocabulary inventory of, first, my children, and then, increasingly, my grandchildren. I'm certain none of my ten grandchildren, now in their twenties and thirties, know a farrago from a virago, an encomium from a panegyric, recondite from arcane, or banter from persiflage. They no longer get courses in Western Civilization or Aesthetics or Creative Writing in college. Their higher education was pretty much in STEM courses — science, technology, engineering, and mathematics — with little exposure to the arts and literature. And the language of their friends and business associates is obviously informal and workaday. The language of texting and emailing is primitive at best, and there is no vocabulary building in most newspaper or TV coverage, with rare exceptions on public TV.

So the only hope for language refinement and vocabulary building for the average Generation Xer is through reading serious novels or serious non-fiction, obviously in private. How much private reading time does a GenX have after work, after gym, after sports, and after TV? Not much, if book sales are any index. In fact, NONE of the generations are building vocabulary and refining their language skills if book sales are any indication. Ask any literary agent or publisher. They might admit that books in print may soon become collectors' items in our twitchy electronic age.

I don't have any illusions about how many of MY

generation could define dissemble or sinecure or anomie or jingo or tocsin or anchorite. But I do believe that a 1950 college graduate left the campus with double the literary vocabulary of a 2013 graduate, and had a far broader cultural education. I recently distributed a speech by the President of Stanford University praising the lifelong value of a liberal arts education. It simply produces a more literate and a more interesting human being than a semi-literate techie

If I were the Educational Emperor of America, I would mandate a return to a curriculum laden with courses in literature, history, and what used to be called Civics. Our semi-literate American public and our dysfunctional, partisan-ridden Federal and State governments could use the makeover.

And a slightly richer vocabulary might make for a richer, prettier, more precise level of communication in the stressed-out American suburbs. But don't hold your breath waiting for it to happen....

2/12/14

A Grotesque Product of Congressional Incompetence

Having just coped with Title 26 of the United States Code Annotated in preparing a 23 page Federal tax return for 2013, I am acutely aware of the one century of accumulated intrigue and duplicity that created the monster known as the U.S. Tax code. Title 26 is 3,387 pages long as written by congress. The IRS has added 13,458 pages of regulations, making a total of 16,845 pages of gobbledygook that a U.S. taxpayer or his CPA is supposed to comply with. The result is an unfunny farce, and every congressman and senator knows it.

The Tax Code is not only voluminous and complex; it's a convoluted patchwork of additions and fixes tacked on for decades because congress kowtowed to special interest angels and never had the courage or political will to overhaul the whole thing. Every honest representative knows that Title 26 is bloated, toxic, and unwieldy. Every IRS agent knows that the average citizen, and often his tax accountant, can't get the tax return 1oo percent right because the code and regulations are simply too complex. And who doesn't know that tens of BILLIONS of dollars of income are not taxed because of loopholes, special treatment, and underreporting.

Nothing in my tax law course in law school prepared me for the intricacies of partnership accounting (especially energy partnerships) or the alternative minimum tax rules, or the record keeping required for stock gifts. And this year I discovered how some stealth provisions of recent tax legislation quietly increased our dividend tax rate to 20 percent and wiped out part of our tax and charitable deductions. Our exemptions went to zero a couple of years ago. And our California income tax rate is now 10.3 percent, so our CA tax bite is a third as large as our Federal.

I guess a messy tax return and a big tax bill do beat the alternative of a low income and a simple tax bill … But if the American political system since WWII had competent, pragmatic leaders instead of lackeys and cowards and temporizers, the month of March would be a lot more like spring for me, and the U.S. national debt would be a lot smaller.

5/8/14

FEEDING THE WOLF PACK

IF YOU EVER HAD any doubt about the origin and matrix of lawyers, you need go no further than to invest in a business or a stock. Or have a nasty fight with a neighbor. Or a spouse. Or a prosecutor. Or other family members eager to share in an estate (picture lions or wolves after a kill…)

What you probably don't realize is that you are dealing indirectly with lawyers all day long. Every product you buy or service you order has a hidden cost of past litigation, or the threat of future litigation, buried in the price. Businesses pay lawyers to anticipate and guard against attacks by other lawyers. This is where the fine print in contracts came from, and the black box warnings on drugs, and the idiot-proof instructions for using products.

The second level of hidden legal costs is the premium the business owner or the corporation pays for liability insurance — in case of attack by customers and their lawyers. What company would operate today without liability insurance, regardless of its product or service? And every time the company needs to borrow money, or raise capital, and especially to issue securities, it suffers the heavy cost of legal due diligence and legal documentation. And the cost of defending litigation if the claim isn't covered by the liability policy.

The third level of behind-the-scenes influence of lawyers is the universal FEAR of litigation, which silently governs the behavior of almost every adult you deal with, a neighbor with a trampoline or a big dog, or a big tree, or a rough sidewalk. A teacher or a coach dealing with attractive teens. A doctor treating you for almost any malady (yes, even your dermatologist). Or a dentist. Or a contractor. Who among them doesn't pay a premium for personal or professional liability insurance — out of fear of a lawsuit for some mishap (or act of God)?

I wrote a small book on the subject of tort litigation, and the need for rational reform, way back in 1990. Like my essays, it was pretty much a monologue after a little local press. But the argument and appeal are as relevant today as they were 24 years ago. The hidden cost of lawyers — born in strife and thriving on conflict — is greater today than it was in 1990, fueled vigorously by the plethora of lawyers created by proprietary and second-tier law schools in the last twenty years. (The joke is that they have special lines for lawyers at the Unemployment Office).

I have a little sign that says the primary function

of a lawyer is to protect his client from others in his profession. Funny, but all too true. Even lawyers love the old saw about a lawyer in a small town starving to death for lack of business — until another lawyer came to town and made them both prosperous....

Two recent items inspired this little discourse. The first was flipping through a couple hundred corporate annual reports during proxy season — March and April. I focus on the per share earnings, and the nature of the corporation's business in the current economic environment (my favorites being natural gas, medical equipment and supplies, and biopharma). But I'm always struck by the voluminous and imaginative "Risk Factors" section of a report. They vary in length from eight to 18 printed pages of text, cataloging every conceivable calamity or downfall or obstacle the company might confront by any possibility. It is thousands of words by a securities lawyer saying, "You were warned, so the risk was yours!" The Risk Factors text is Exhibit A to the theme that a lawyer's first job is to foresee trouble, then his second job is to ward off anyone harmed by it....

The other current development is a well-financed initiative by the trial lawyers of California to amend the Business and Professions Code to raise the 1976 limit on pain and suffering damages in medical malpractice litigation from $250,000 to $1,000,000. This is obviously being vigorously opposed by the insurance industry and their Republican allies, who have successfully established verdict limits in medical cases in other states, like Florida and Virginia. The odds of passage are probably 50-50, balanced by those who have sympathy for medically damaged plaintiffs against those who dislike or resent lawyers in general.

We have two good lawyers in the family, so I have to muffle my opinion of lawyers in general because of their good deeds. In fact, Kenny was wounded financially by Virginia's statutory limit on medical malpractice awards a couple of years ago, when his jury asked the judge if they could award MORE than $1,950,000 in his serious case. The judge said no — that's the law.

So respect lawyers all you wish. All I'm saying is that there are too many of them for the good of society, and that you should realize how much you are paying for them....

4/23/14

THE SECOND HOME SYNDROME:
How We Got Cured

POOR PEOPLE DON'T EVEN think about a second or vacation home. Rich people probably already have a beach house or a mountain chalet. But I think that middle class Americans fall into three categories: those who would like a vacation retreat, those who did inherit or buy a condo, bungalow, or cabin, and those who had one and unloaded it.

We fall in the third category, and will stay there. Fifteen or sixteen years ago we were making frequent trips to two favorite idylls, Jackson Lake, Wyoming and Southern Vermont, my childhood haunt. We stayed at Jackson Lake Lodge in Wyoming and at an early girlfriend's home in Rutland, Vermont. Each junket involved two plane rides and a rental car. Orange County Airport-Salt Lake City-Jackson took only four hours door-to-door, but O.C.-Chicago-Albany was more like eight hours, including an hour and a half drive from Albany to Rutland. But each trip was worth it — cutthroat trout and breakfast rides in Wyoming, old haunts, greenery, and two early girlfriends in Southern Vermont.

Real property in Jackson, Wyoming was then, and still is, priced out of sight. But prices in Vermont villages were then rational, and the price on a modern, six bedroom ski house on six acres near Londonderry, Vermont was irresistible, partly because it had been struck by lightning and still had some shattered glass in the living room.

The potential, and the view, were outstanding and we could picture some great family get-togethers there. We had five members in Virginia and 13 or 14 in California, many of them skiers and hikers. The lightning had hit a tree next to the house, then bounced a little, shattering glass, but did no structural damage.

I suspect that the lightning strike shook up the Long Island family that owned it as a second home, and maybe they wearied of the drive or the kids grew up and played elsewhere. In any case, we closed the deal for just under six figures, picked the glass out if the living room sofa, moved it downstairs to the game room, bought a couple of new appliances and a new master bedroom mattress, and had a friend install a new stairway from the parking area with railroad ties. "Forestport" was now open for business, meaning friends and relatives only, any time they wished.

Over the next five years we had one big family reunion at Forestport, spend a few long weekends there with friends, and were happy to see Ken and Melanie bring up friends from Virginia during the summer. Then we sold a half interest in Forestport to a Connecticut couple who rented it for ski excursions, so we had almost all of our investment back and had someone closer to deal with repairs, like porch damage from snow runoff. Our excursions took us to the U.K., Alaska, the B.V.I., and Hawaii, so Forestport became more of a distant problem than a retreat. Why pay taxes and repair bills when you can simply reserve and walk away from DIFFERENT beautiful vista in Scotland, the Caribbean, Wyoming, and Kauai?

We sold our remaining half of Forestport to the Zeiglers, paid a little capital gain tax to the State of Vermont, and decided never again to tie ourselves to a single lovely retreat when there are so many others ready and waiting. We no longer have to do any housekeeping or cooking in Vermont. We no longer worry about a blight or climate change killing off the sugar maples. We can fly to Hartford and be in Room 2 at The Landgrove Inn (near Weston) by nightfall if we wish.

But Norway, Little Dix Bay, Costa Rica, and Poipu all beckon, as does penthouse suite #1018 on the Crystal Symphony. We see our friends and kids retreating repeatedly to their second homes. Better them than us. We're cured. We like two things when we leave home: leisure and variety....

5/5/14

The V.A. Is Only Exhibit A

WHEN THE SMOKE HAS cleared — no doubt after the November elections — you will probably be told that the V.A. went rogue because of a couple of factors. First, it has been overwhelmed by the tens of thousands of victims of the two disastrous Bush wars. And, second, it has been grossly underfunded since 2000 by an economy-minded congress whose priority is defense and investigations, not infrastructure and "socialized medicine."

Both claims are true. But I submit to you that the malfunction of the V.A. and the corruption in its management are far from an isolated case of government gone wrong.

Take a look at a few other branches of the U.S. government. The IRS has been criticized for political discrimination. The SEC is under fire again for its pathetic record of policing, or should I say non-policing (Madoff and countless others). The INS draws fire for its rogue agents and misplaced weapons. The FDA is damned both for its delays in approval and for flawed

118

approvals leading to dangerous drugs. The USPS is belittled for slow service and cost overruns. And let's not forget our wonderful congress, full of political hacks financed by PACs and lobbies, or libertarian ideologues who yearn for an America that isn't coming back.

I think the two primary bugaboos of U.S. government are size and complexity. Size alone begets a problem of management, especially from the top. You can't see the bottom from the top. And who is lucky enough to have a full cadre of competent and honest middle managers? Not much of a chance. Sheer size alone makes it impossible to manage a behemoth like the U.S. government without endless snafus and crises.

But the other jinx in the machine is complexity. Huge size alone produces some degree of complexity. Technological evolution tends to add complexity. And political beneficence adds the next ingredient: as operational problems develop with growth and social conflict, politicians craft new programs and systems to solve new problems. U.S. society is vastly more complex than it was even fifty years ago. And government obviously incorporates, if not increases, the complexity of the American socio-economic-political structure.

Size and complexity would be challenge enough to discourage any serene, rational human from entering government service. But I offer the following precept as a guarantee of continuing and endless crises and scandals in all major branches of U.S. government.

Complexity breeds corruption! How could we have tens of thousands of tax cheats if we had a simple tax code and a well-funded enforcement bureau? How could we have efficient operation of hundreds of regional V.A. centers when they are under-funded, geographically scattered, and not under close management? How could the SEC police a financial empire so vast and complex that even the bankers don't know exactly what the law is this week? How can the FDA make increasing numbers of extremely complex biochemical decisions with a limited budget and staff?

Add a third element to size and complexity and you have what I would call a media delight. Avarice is that third element and it thrives on both size and complexity because both size and complexity keep corruption out of the limelight. As long as you have a dozen or more homo sapiens on your staff, you have fertile ground for some form of self-serving corruption. Size and complexity provide the necessary smoke and mirrors for connivers — if management is too distant, too dull, or too distracted. Avarice is a virus in large organizations that thrives on complexity or lack of oversight. It's the mother lode for prosecutors, congressional committees, auditors, and the media.

The combination of size, complexity, and avarice makes me wonder why any rational and successful intellectual would ever run for federal (or even state) office. They must have a greater appetite for stress, conflict, and vilification than I do. And a greater need for ego gratification.

6/1/14

Postscript: The V.A. mess reminds me of the following observation by Rudyard Kipling more than a century ago.

> *God and the soldier we adore,*
> *In times of danger, not before.*
> *The danger passed, and all things righted,*
> *God is forgotten and the soldier slighted....*

How Do You Deal With One of Them?

Do you know anyone who:

1. Basically distrusts and slanders government, especially the Federal government?

2. Resents and distrusts foreigners, especially illegal immigrants?

3. Likes guns and has the opinion that the Second Amendment prohibits any regulation of guns?

4. Believes that women are out of control and should stick to raising kids and running the home?

5. Is no stranger to violence and flies a Don't Tread On Me flag, or claims to be a Sovereign or a member of a militia?

6. Thinks that most of the poor are lazy or indolent and happy to rely on government handouts?

7. Listens to a lot of talk radio?

8. Thinks that Rush Limbaugh, Sean Hannity, and Glen Beck are right on target and telling it like it is?

9. Believes that the end justifies the means and that dirty tricks (a la Karl Rove) are called for in fighting the bleeding heart liberals and their big government?

10. Accepts the mantra about a free (meaning unregulated) market being the only path to prosperity, and that wealth will trickle down (a la Reagan) from above if taxes are slashed and big government is dismantled?

11. Is insular and fixed in attitudes and opinions, and bellicose about higher education, the "Liberal Media," the United Nations, and any International pacts or accords?

12. Is against any form of birth control or abortion, or even family planning if the government is in any way involved — but also condemns government programs aimed at abandoned, neglected, or abused children?

13. Denies that there is any threat of global warming or climate change due to man's activity, so is against any government control of emissions or ecological degradation?

If you do know someone who meets many or most of those criteria, my advice would be to avoid wasting any time trying to convert or enlighten them. In my case, I avoid any socializing and try to avoid any contact. Because to me — a one-time Taft Republican — an American radical right-winger is a kissing cousin of either a Klansman or a neo-Nazi. So the word "shun" comes to mind.

6/22/14

SHILLS UNLIMITED: Pretenders Come In All Shapes and Sizes

I WATCH AS LITTLE commercial TV as possible, but even CNBC and PBS and KCET are loaded with commercials. Since I'm almost always on "mute" — with captions — I don't have to listen to the blather of a million shills. But I too often watch their histrionic hustling of commercial products and wonder if any one of them has EVER tried or used the wares they're puffing. And I wonder if they feel the slightest pangs of remorse while grinning, mugging, and demonstrating for dollars over a product or service they know little or nothing about.

Maralys and I once attended one of Brad's video shoots in Irvine and watched a well-dressed model type rattle off her script lines over and over until Brad was satisfied with the scene. She then got her check and departed. The shoot setup and production took a couple of hours, but the scene was probably twenty seconds long.

I wonder if that on-call actress felt in any way

like a prostitute. She delivered image and lines instead of flesh, but she knew as little about Allergan and its pharmaceutical products as a harlot knows about a one-time customer's life history or even marital status. Yet the TV or video actress who fakes fulfillment, delight, horror, or satisfaction is a respected, or at least honorable, American performer, while the strumpet is reviled and rejected (if not stoned), by respectable society.

Why the difference, all down through the ages? Each is a presentable, if not attractive, woman pretending to be something or someone she's not. The actress pretends a persona, or to treasure a product, or to have certain emotions. The prostitute my simulate affection, or passion, but is basically just lending body parts and performing bodily functions. One gets big checks and awards. The other gets a fee, dismissal, maybe even arrest.

It must go back to some early notion of female body parts being sacred and prime or cardinal, whereas behavioral hypocrisy was endemic, therefore venial. Religion took it from there, and the law followed on.

America is a land built on generous natural resources, energy, innovation, hybrid vigor, and ego. All great assets. But it's also a commercial world built on pretence and duplicity. That's where the hustlers, hucksters, scammers, con artists, and snake oil salesmen come in. And that's where the TV and trade show shills also come in. They're gatherers for the peddlers.

But they're only pretending, playacting, not

sharing body parts. So I guess they're OK. But not for me. I don't relish any of the various forms of pretense. But I suspect that the prostitutes may be the least hypocritical variety of pretenders.

7/1/14

A Crapshoot Twice a Day...

I DON'T QUALIFY FOR Gamblers Anonymous, but the fact is that I'm involved in a crapshoot every day of the year. In fact, two crapshoots most days.

On business days, I watch CNBC to see how our stock portfolio is doing. I probably make five or six trades by phone in an average week. Bonds are too boring — stodgy — and I don't trust gold, commodities, mutual funds, or annuities. I do my own trading and break all the rules on cash-debt-equity proportionality, so I guess that makes me a true crapshooter at the Wall Street tables. But so far, so good. In forty years I rode out the dips and made good bets on energy, pharmaceuticals, and medical supplies. I'm way ahead of the "house" and can ride out any corrections that may come along. But any CFA watching me along the way would have certified me for membership in Gamblers Anonymous.

The other crapshoot is a lot scarier, and takes place each and every day. It involves my body and my brain, every vital organ. They're all at risk every day and

I'm in no position to evaluate that risk because I'm neither an award-winning biochemist or pharmacophysiologist. I take a statin-dyslipidemic, I take an NSAID. I take a blood glucose regulator. I take Xanthophyll. I take a multivitamin-mineral supplement. I take two man made vitamins. And I take some niacin.

These are all biochemicals. In the business of pharmacology they are GRAS drugs — generally regarded as safe. But are they REALLY safe? Thalidomide was GRAS — until all the birth defects showed up (it's in use again, for a different purpose...). VIOXX was GRAS — until it was recalled and cost Merck hundreds of millions ... Bextra, another NSAID, was GRAS — until it was pulled. Bendectin was a popular anti-morning sickness drug — until it was pulled and caused a huge class action suit for birth defects (later discredited). FenPhen was a popular weight loss drug — until it was found to be dangerous and resulted in a $3.75 billion settlement. Avandia was pulled because of cardiovascular risk — then reapproved.

All of those drugs had been through years of field trials, three different stages. All were GRAS — for awhile. So since human biophysiology is so complex, so arcane, how safe can we feel taking drugs that haven't been pulled yet?

If you read the manufacturer's inserts that come with your drugs, you'll be a nervous wreck. The inserts may as well have been — and maybe were — written by Philadelphia lawyers. The list of side effects and complications is terrifying. The incompatibility problem with other drugs is alarming. And beware of drug interactions! If patients read these warnings — which they don't — they probably would never take the drugs. They are so dire it's a wonder there isn't a skull and crossbones at the head of the insert.

I even get warnings about drugs in the mail. Public opinion puts out periodic warnings on drugs and medical equipment in popular use. Then there's a Dr. Sidney Wolfe who promotes his *Good Drugs, Bad Drugs* book and newsletters. He damns a lot of the drugs still in use, including Celebrex and Voltarin, and he reminds us of his warnings on drugs that were later pulled.

So where am I, taking eight biopharmacologics daily? I'm dizzy, that's where I am. The cane is for that problem, not knee pain ... But I'm mobile, despite severe osteo (genes from both parents). I passed my stress echocardiogram last week. (I guess the calcium plaque is on the coronary artery walls, not in the lumen....) I'm mentally alert, if not morally straight. So, whether because of the drugs or in spite of them, I'm cruising along OK for age 87.

So I'll continue the pharmacologic crapshoot until someone has a better idea. I hope I win that game as well as I have the stock market crapshoot.

7/15/14

Live Free or Die and Other Libertarian Claptrap

A FAVORITE BATTLE CRY of the American right wing is Live Free or Die, apparently signifying open defiance with a clenched fist. What this shibboleth really boils down to is "Don't try to regulate me or I'll die fighting you." And what the various criminals who have those words tattooed on their bodies mean is "Try to capture me and one of us is going to end up dead."

Maybe the last time you saw those four words was on a New Hampshire license plate, since it's the N.H. state motto. Having grown up in Vermont, very much a sister state to N.H., I know that not everyone in New Hampshire is a libertarian simpleton. But a great many simpletons outside New Hampshire have embraced the motto as a battle cry against the evil government that they see as intent on smothering or incarcerating them. Think of the "Militia" crazies, The "Freemen," the "Sovereign" citizens, the religious cult leaders, the sundry hate groups, and finally the most hardened criminals in our prisons.

Some of the Tea Party fringe of the Republican Party also embrace simplistic shibboleths like " Live Free or Die" and "Don't Tread on Me." Look for that theme on their flags, bumper stickers, and campaign placards. They like to think of themselves as modern-day descendants of the American patriots who rejected British imperial tyranny. But the U.S. right wing wouldn't know governmental tyranny if it stared them in the face. They have grown up in one of the freest societies on the planet, but are spoiling to reject regulation by government in a manner reminiscent of the spoiled child's revolt against domination by a frustrated parent.

Carry the simple-minded "Live Free or Die" to its logical conclusion. But you can't do it without defining "free." If "free" means with no physical or societal restraints at all, "die" would be a fairly rapid alternative… Utopian societies always disintegrate rapidly because unregulated humans very quickly get on each other's nerves and provocation can lead to the death alternative. Sylvester Stallone is no philosopher, but Rocky hit the nail on the head when he said "If you believe that people will do the right thing, get rid of the police for 24 hours and see what happens…."

Until you define "free," the discussion is pretty much hopeless. Which makes a lot of American flag waving anthems practically worthless." The Price of Liberty is Eternal Vigilance." Another charming adage, but "liberty" begs definition and "vigilance" speaks of observation without action.

I don't do bumper stickers or campaign posters, or even membership pins, but if I did I would never go for anything as inane as "Live Free or Die" or "Don't Tread on Me." It would have to be something like "Don't Let The Billionaires Buy the Senate," or "Libertarians are Spoiled Brats," or "Vote No on Gridlock'. But as I say, I don't do slogans or bumper stickers....

8/5/15

ANOTHER OUTLANDISH DECISION:
What Was She Thinking?

A U.S. DISTRICT COURT Judge has opened Pandora's Box in college athletics. She basically said that college athletes should share in the big pot produced by big-time college football and basketball. Hopefully, a Federal appellate court will reverse that slapdash decision out of hand, not only because the NCAA violently opposes it on appeal, but because of the innumerable reasons the decision was asinine.

Among them are:

1. Only seven of the big time college football programs actually make money. No question the TV and radio sports broadcasters make money. The Coliseum and Rose Bowl operators make money. The Vegas bookmakers make money. The sporting equipment manufacturers make money. The concessionaires make money. And even a few celebrated college stars probably make a little money — sub Rosa and illegally.

But none of those moneymakers pay the coaches or buy the uniforms or maintain college arenas or pay the scholarships. The schools fielding big name teams that are TV darlings no doubt show a profit even after paying their coaches six or seven figures. But thus far the media report that almost all college athlete programs operate at a loss.

2. So if prominent college athletes can now demand a salary, do they sign with the highest bidder? How do the small colleges compete with that, especially when they are already losing money in the stadium and field house? Do the athletes demand a full scholarship plus a salary? Do private schools with rich alumni keep all the best athletes away from the state schools that already have huge budget problems?

3. The lawsuit producing the goofy decision was brought by a male UCLA basketball player who starred years ago. What about the minor sports like tennis, swimming, soccer, gymnastics, Lacrosse? Those programs don't make money even for private schools like USC and Stanford. Does the best 18 year old swimmer or tennis player in California demand not only a full scholarship, but a

salary? Fat chance!

4. What abut Title IX and the girls' sports programs? If none of the women's programs make money, are the female star athletes still entitled to some compensation if the male football and basketball players receive salaries at Florida State, Alabama, Texas, Oklahoma, USC, UCLA, and Stanford? Good luck on that girls....

5. In another decision, the Northwestern football team has been given an OK to unionize. If they do, and don't reach an agreement with the Northwestern administration, are they willing to go on strike and cancel the season? Good luck on that when the alumni hold their emergency meeting....

As if college athletics wasn't messy enough, with drugs, cheating, and illegal payments, here we go to labor conflicts and salary wars. Unless the NCAA gets Judge Claudia Wilkens' decision reversed, and the Northwestern football team can't get organized as a union, I think I'll skip the sports news for a couple of years and trash all season ticket solicitations.

8/18/14

Brief Encounters that Whet an Untamed Appetite

SHIPS THAT PASS IN the night may or may not have been interesting. But beautiful women who pass in plain view, usually too fast, are another matter.

One would think that after spawning a clan of six children, ten grandchildren, and eleven great grand children, an aging male would be immune to the loveliness and charms of the female sex. Thankfully, not the case. Actually, not anything like the case.

In fact, now that I think about it, I am far more susceptible to a vision of female loveliness at age 87 than I was as an intense, self-assured scholar in his early twenties. Then there was sex appeal if the shape and persona were attractive, but there was missing an element of mystique, seduction, or forbidden pleasure that developed with age. As I discovered the diversity and complexity of the mature females, that revelation, accompanied by the unavailability of a lively, lovely woman to a conspicuously married man, made the chance encounter with a nymph ever more affecting.

It would be hard to describe a female you got to know well as irresistible, or even intriguing, but I can recall a half dozen chance encounters with women who seemed irresistible on first view but remain only a proverbial vision of loveliness as the contact dissolved. A brief encounter may develop into a flaming romance in a movie or play, but in real life only the vision remains — with the question of what might have been....

I occasionally recall the few instances in seven decades where the appearance and appeal of an unknown woman left an indelible impression of loveliness and a regret that we would never meet again. What was it about her that stuck in my mind and made me wish I had extended the contact? Not just her beauty, though it was obvious. Was it sweetness, which is so rare, and ethereal (and usually transitory)? Was it openness? Vitality, what I call life force? Or was it a subtle but simmering sexuality, something you don't see in your social circles?

Whatever it was, it was alluring, both to the eyes and to the mind. There was that beautiful and charming German girl named Ulrike on that Eurailpass train in Germany. There was that lovely wife at another table in a South Lake Tahoe restaurant after a day of skiing.

There was that Pennsylvania wife on a solo trip to Vermont, hiking alone on the trail above Mt. Tabor, and anxious to chat with a California husband who was already late for dinner in Rutland (I fished too long.)

And there was that fresh young beauty who approached me on a large rock above Jenny Lake in the Tetons. I joined her and her mother down the trail, but we parted suddenly without name or address. And there was that vibrant, unmissable beauty ahead of us in the check in line at the MGM Grand in Vegas. God, who was she, and who was lucky enough to room with her in that Mecca?

The last brief almost-encounter with an intriguing Lorelei was right here in Tustin, at Souplantation, of all places. She and her young daughter started to sit by me, but then moved to join another young mother and her daughter. Maralys arrived and I told her my assessment of the woman, which caused Maralys to pause by her to see her face. "See what I mean?" was my comment as we departed, never to meet or see again a woman I wish we knew.

I suppose it's common and forgivable for adult married males (and females) to lick their lips over glamorous actresses (or actors) on the screen, but somehow it's not so painful there to walk away without even a physical encounter. In fact, only three females I ever saw on screen made me want to present myself. Start with Merle Oberon, a Eurasian beauty in *Wuthering Heights*. Then there was a lush Swedish girl in *One Summer of Happiness* sixty years ago. Her name was Ulla Jacobsson and who could resist her, naked or otherwise? Then there was Jennifer O'Neill, basically a beautiful model, as an unfaithful but luscious wife in *Summer of 42*. Who didn't envy that 15-year-old boy?

I wonder if Maralys will be surprised, when she prints this out upstairs on her computer (I type — she prints). I haven't mentioned all of these brief encounters (and "sightings"), to her but she knows me well after 66 years and hopefully appreciates both my honesty and my unavailability....

9/10/14

So as we see it here on Beverly Glen Drive, our thoroughly enjoyable lifestyle here in Southern California is being threatened both from within — by radical Republicanism — and from without, by radical Muslim terrorism. Oh well, in the meanwhile let's focus on the here and now, not the there and then. And hope that God, Allah, Buddha, karma, or just plain kismet works on the problem....

9/27/14

You Can't Say it, but You Can See it: Race Matters

ONE OF THE IRONIES in this supposedly color blind society is that almost everyone is aware of race but no one is supposed to talk about it. You aren't supposed to notice that almost all pro basketball stars are "black," which means black or brown. Increasingly so in pro football, including even quarterbacks. And coaches, pro or college, football or basketball.

Then there's show biz. Blacks have long since thrived in comedy, a cathartic preferable to violence. Cosby and Redd Fox and Sherman Hemsley ("George Jefferson") led the way in sitcoms. Black game show hosts followed. Black or brown late night talk show hosts can't be far behind.

And TV advertisers have increasingly targeted the growing percentage of black and brown Americans. You rarely see a TV group ad now that doesn't include at least one member of a so-called "minority group." The advertising industry doesn't talk about race; it merely recognizes it and acts on it, just like corporate employers and college admission staffs do.

The one area where Americans are quick to talk about race is in the criminal justice system. Oh yes, the prisons have a grossly disproportionate number of black and Latino inmates — presumably because of racial prejudice in the police ranks, the courts, and the jury room. I'm not sure it's that simple, but who would have the courage to suggest other causes? That would smack of — yes, racism....

Because of the national guilt complex over the evils of centuries of slavery, no one is going to brave a demographic, neurological, or sociological analysis of racial trends and differences in the land of the Level Playing Field. Which orthopedic surgeon will opine that blacks rarely excel in swimming because their skeletons are heavier? Or that Pacific Islanders make good linemen because they don't feel much pain? Or that blacks lean toward sports and show biz because they are the gateway to money and glory for less gifted students?

I have no doubt about the fact that the U.S. playing field isn't level for blacks and Latinos. But I don't buy slavery here 150 years ago or tyranny in poor Latin countries of origin as the prime causes. Other sociological or physiological factors are at work.

I don't know what they are, but I wish the civil rights, populist, and egalitarian stalwarts in the U.S. didn't so intimidate American scientists and sociologists that no Gunnar Myrdal(*) would ever be willing to do an objective study of race in America today.

10/5/14

*Gunnar Myrdal, a Swede, won the Nobel Peace Prize in 1944 for an analysis of the "American Negro" problem.

Up One River, Across Another, and Down One

Yoʻll no doubt get rave reports about our two-week, three river, five country odyssey. And they're right. Not only did we have 17 days of good flights, good food, good lectures, and good entertainment, but we defied all odds by having no accidents, no illnesses, no theft losses, and no lost luggage … How do you beat those odds?

Brad would have loved that trip. Food, variety, and adventure. Even the river-side bike rides. Tracy made the 100 percent correct decision not to go on this one. Meanwhile she established national ascendancy in both pickleball *and* tennis …

A history buff would have loved this trip. Our guides, both Tauck and local, were walking encyclopedias and we were BOMBARDED with names and dates between the eleventh and nineteenth centuries. In contrast with the U.S., Europeans seem to love and hang onto the past. World War II was the latest event I heard mentioned in two weeks of lectures (except

Maralys' talk on the ship....)

You would all have been proud of the Whirlybird Cycling Wills Wizards. We won three of the four contests on the ship, based on both ingenuity and information. We won caps, scarves, and aprons. It was an invincible gang of six. The Tauck staff will remember us for awhile, including the 21-mile bike ride through vineyards on the Danube in Austria.

I didn't use my camera and I don't think Kenny has owned one for twenty years. I hope Chris and Betty-Jo have some good ones I can get printed. Memories fade. Photos don't.

I've written to the CEO of Tauck to tell him why we will always check first with Tauck for any river or extended land trip. We first learned why they are the best on two heli-hiking trips thirty years ago.

I'm beating Maralys to the punch with my "blog."

11/15/14

The Holidays Again? After Only a Few Months? or so it Seems

Somewhere in the course of eight years of college courses, I ran across a theory that might explain the fact that time moves faster as you age. It was called Normal Negligence, a bad name to a lawyer, but it observed that familiarity breeds not only contempt, but also weak or transient memory traces in the brain. This results in less accumulation of memory of mundane and routine activity in our lives. Lack of memory means lack of sense of time. So here we are at Thanksgiving again....

However, despite Brad's death, we did add some very nice memory tracks in 2014, aided as always with photos. You'll see visual traces of Jamie Worley's wedding to Mike Toole, a Caribbean honeymoon cruise after that, Lauren's graduation from Nursing School, Dane's graduation from UCLA, a great week on the Big Island after that, and a three river-five country-two-week trip through central Europe on the M.S. Treasures. That's more than our share of memory traces for one year, because all three trips were exceptional, so we should rest on our laurels for awhile.

After a week in Germany, we could see why Germany has now passed the U.S. as the most "popular" country in the world. And if the U.S. infrastructure and congress both continue to deteriorate, I would expect the U.S. to drop down a few more notches. Some of the countries in northern Europe are both stable and progressive, whereas the U.S. now seems to be retrogressive, partly because of government gridlock.

It's hard to maintain equanimity if you follow the news as much as we do. The Muslim threat has been rising ever since our stupid invasion and destruction of Iraq in 2003 and the Muslims have two advantages over the so-called Christian world — greater numbers and lack of fear of death.

I still can't believe we don't have suicide bombers in the U.S., but I don't see how the FBI, CIA, NSA, and TSA can prevent them forever. Those agencies have a tough time thwarting terrorists in a huge country blessed with closely guarded individual freedoms and harboring smoldering racial and religious tension (witness Ferguson and Detroit). Hopefully they are diligent in monitoring 1) the Internet, 2) the phones of radical Muslims, and 3) sales of chemicals and other bomb components through manufacturers, hardware stores, and drug stores.

As for a war with Russia, I don't think that even

the saber-rattling Republicans are that suicidal; we haven't WON a war since 1945, we've lost four or five of them, a nuclear war would be asinine as well as gruesome, and no one can beat Russia in a land war (ask the Germans). So Obama has the only solution for thugs like Putin, sanctions and shame. If they don't work, good luck GOP!

As for Obama's dismal popularity ratings, I think his intellect is probably his undoing. Ford, Reagan, and Bush proved that intellect is not a requirement for the White House. Wilson, Carter, and Obama proved that it's a handicap in American politics. Barack Obama belonged on the Supreme Court, not in the White House. Maybe he'll acknowledge that in his next book.

I spend part of every weekday watching Wall Street and have come to the conclusion that Wall Street has very little connection to Main Street. And Wall Street loves government gridlock. All three market indexes hit records before November 6 and have risen even higher since, expecting nothing but odium and enmity between congress and the White House for two years. Gridlock means no legislation. And no legislation means no new regulations or taxes (not to mention bridges or highways). And probably no anti-trust enforcement or DJ threat to Wall Street, big banks, hedge funds, or mergers. Congratulations investors. Beware consumers....

The overarching threat to our future continues

to be population growth, and all the other nemeses are corollaries of it (water, food, air and water pollution, deforestation, civil unrest, and poverty). If you think traffic, potholes, homelessness, hungry children, ghettoes, and favelas are bad with 7 ½ billion humans, wait until you see them at 10 billion if present birth rates continue, especially in the Third World.

I think the next Nobel Prize should go not to an astrophysicist or a tech wizard, but to a biologist or physiologist who produces a birth control injectable or consumable that is inexpensive to make and easy to distribute. Someone or something (other than a nuclear holocaust) has to counteract the religious and political forces mitigating against worldwide birth control and family planning. Has everyone forgotten the first bill that born-again George W. Bush signed in 2000? It was called the Mexico City bill and banned U.S. funds for birth control and family planning, not only in the U.S., but overseas as well. How many unwanted children in the third world owe their existence to a reformed alcoholic and his evangelical base?

I'm happy to read recently that Melinda Gates is calling for a new easy-to-administer birth control system. We've been waiting for bright philanthropists like her to focus on the underlying problem and not just medical remediation in poor, overpopulated nations in Africa and Asia. In the African, Asian, and Arab countries women are underpowered and victims of excessive pregnancies. How better to empower them than to give them cheap, effective birth control and family planning (not to mention drivers' licenses).

In our own country, those who have the courage to follow the news (I don't mean Fox) must be pained about the number of homeless, especially children, and poor who go to bed hungry at night. They are virtually out of sight of the American upper and middle classes, but they are there, in the U.S., and in the millions. A lot of them were unwanted and then neglected or rejected children.

And yet — this is what I call the conservative schizophrenia — the same religious and political right wing, Tea Party and others, who resent food stamps and unemployment insurance extensions and other so-called handout programs are the same group that violently opposes abortion and government funded birth control and family planning. Try to figure that one out. Someone ought to think it through for them. If you are going to protect unwanted pregnancies, get real about the odds that the results may end up in social programs or more prisons.

Only a friend or curious observer has read this far, so you know better than to expect a Jolly Joe Christmas greeting from me. I avoid Christmas crowds, Christmas shopping, canned Christmas carols, and syrupy Christmas letters, at least by me. But I do hope that your 2014 was accident, illness, and bankruptcy free, and that you continue to enjoy the blessings of a free and bountiful society, at least for most of us.

12/1/14

P.S. Tracy is a champion not only in tennis and pickle ball, but in courage and recovery as well. We know that she'll make a good recovery after a very tough, almost brutal, year. We've all been through tragedy in this family and life always goes on for the remarkable swarm of survivors.

Part 4

A Treasure Trove Of Talent...

B UT WHERE IS IT headed? In the course of three days we have watched a virtuoso violinist, a master pianist, and a 14-year-old triple threat who set a packed theater afire after being called in five days earlier to replace the injured star. And the 14-year-old boy was surrounded by at least 25 hoofers, all of whom could sing and act, as well as dance, in a dazzling production worthy of Broadway.

So much talent in just three days, two of them in a private home, and not one of the group a name we had ever heard before. The same thing happens time after time, on stages in Costa Mesa, La Mirada, Long Beach, and Fullerton. There must be thousands of artists in Orange and L.A. counties whose names we don't know but who can dazzle you with world class music, dancing, and acting. Only a fraction will make it to New York or London — or even make a middle class living out of their artistic talent.

We relish the amazing pool of artistic talent in

Southern California, but we can't miss the contrast as we watch literally hundreds of football players in Sunday playoffs, each of which is strong and agile and aggressive — and makes six or seven figures per year. Many of their names would be known to our grandkids, if not our kids. And all of them will be living in nice homes with investment portfolios as they limp through middle age (with or without chronic traumatic encephalopathy).

Meanwhile, most of the musicians and actors and dancers will be working for scale on weekends, waiting for a call from their agent, or toiling away at non-glamorous jobs. A few, precious few, will make a living playing off-Broadway stages all over the U.S.; there are a lot of community theater stages in the U.S. But even those performers usually have backup jobs like voiceover, commercials, or studio teaching.

We keep seeing actors, singers, musicians, and dancers who deserve to be famous. We're still waiting. I have the programs from over fifty years of performances on Orange County, Los Angeles, Las Vegas, and Tahoe stages. There are a few familiar names in them; Jay Leno, John Denver, Steve Martin in their early years. But most of the hundreds of headliners are doing something else now, replaced by an endless stream of new talent, like the 14-year-old from Florida who nailed Billy Elliot on Saturday night. The four of us have to believe he will be a household name in a very few years, since he is a charming triple threat. We hope history is wrong this time.

And I'm also betting on the 27-year-old Indian violinist, a Stanford alum, who played a complex 15-minute Bach piece on par with any violinist in the world. We kept asking ourselves — are we in Symphony Hall, Kennedy Center, or a friend's living room? If there is any market for a violin virtuoso in a sports-obsessed society, she'll be famous someday.

1/18/15

How Would You Like to Be an American Policeman?

WE KNOW THAT THIS country is politically polarized, to the point where congress barely functions and the federal government is partially paralyzed. But there's another polarization developing that could get even messier and closer to home.

I'm referring to the growing assault on American police departments by a growing coalition of challengers. The first line of police enemies is obviously the quietest and least organized, namely the criminal element of society. But the groups making the noise and threatening the very status and effectiveness of police in the U.S. are two minority groups, Hispanics and African-Americans, and their growing legion of sympathizers and advocates, chiefly activist "liberals" and libertarians.

These groups have successfully programmed the American public to believe not only that the police are essentially hostile to the two minority groups but that, once arrested, the minorities do not get a fair shake in

American courts. And they are now campaigning to prove that many or most American cops are prone to brutalize, if not kill, minority perpetrators when challenged or confronted.

Ferguson, Staten Island, and Cleveland are all Exhibit A against police in general. And the pressure is on police everywhere to go slow on deadly force, not to use it unless the officer fears for his own life, and to use as little force as possible in subduing an arrestee.

This is all right and good — unless you're the policeman dealing with a miscreant who has already spent time in prison and who will take any action possible to avoid capture. Ex-cons in the process of being arrested and returned to prison are in no mood to submit quietly, and if they're armed, a cop's life is definitely on the line. The problem comes in determining in a few seconds whether the subject is armed or just making rapid motions. The inevitable question being debated in the press and in disciplinary hearings everywhere is whether the officer truly and reasonably believed that his life itself was in danger. That's a pretty tough question for commissioners, judges, jurors, and media commentators to answer when they've never in their lives been confronted by a dangerous and desperate criminal.

The problem is that there has been so much police brutality and unjustified use of deadly force that the activists are moving the pendulum so far in the other direction that police personnel now feel persecuted and a little paranoid. The metropolitan police departments in the U.S. are now stung by the criticism and grappling with the problem. They're considering increased police cams, increased arrest training, and more backup on confrontations, chases, and arrests.

But it's the individual cop on the beat that worries me. Is it any wonder that he's dispirited, if not depressed? He's caught between dangerous thugs and psychopaths in the street and hostile second guessers on the inside, in the press, in the disciplinary hearings, and in the courtroom. He's confronted by mobs of hostile demonstrators in the street , having to avoid injury there as well. Yet he's told to go out on patrol as a goodwill ambassador and to undo all the bad press police have gotten every time a black or a Mexican youth is shot.

Good luck to all the police chiefs in metropolitan U.S. areas. They have a tough job ahead of them when every arrest and police shooting is sure to be put under the microscope of both criminal law and public opinion. But pity the poor cop, in danger in the street, under attack in the press, second guessed in the courtroom, and having to battle political budget hawks over his salary and his pension.

If he feels abused or abandoned in 2015 America, it's easy to see why. The next time you read about a work stoppage called "blue flu', or a strange decline in the number of citations and arrests in some jurisdiction, or a slower response to a 911 call, don't try too hard to figure out why. Your hallowed keepers of the peace can only take so much abuse. They're being attacked from all sides and aren't happy about it. The question is, what can they do about it?

1/24/15

WHAT DOES YOUR SEAT
SAY ABOUT YOU?

I WONDER IF IT's only attorneys, board members, and teachers who notice a geographic homing pattern when it comes to seating, whether at a meeting, a deposition, or in class. Even if the gathering is only one day long, people will head for the same seats after the break and after lunch.

There are reasons for this in depositions or school classes or government councils or corporate board meetings. A teacher wants geographic orientation for familiarity and organization. Attorneys at a deposition pretty much locate in the order of their status in the case and their role in the deposition (counsel for the deponent, counsel setting the deposition, principal versus peripheral defendants, etc.).

Corporate board members locate in terms of rank and seniority from the Chairman outward. Government council members have assigned seats in a row, as do panel members. Even church and organization members tend to sit in the same portion of the sanctuary or meeting room or chambers, if not the same seats.

For example, ever since we left the choir years ago, I don't know why Maralys and I have always sat on the left side of our church sanctuary, in the front half. It's simply our area, a habitual orientation. Other members seem to have homing instincts in there, too. Not specific seats or rows, but general vicinity.

We rarely subject ourselves to movie theaters these days, not being gluttons for punishment and TV being so versatile and comfortable. Our seating for our TV viewing at home is fixed also, set in stone.

We don't see where most people sleep, but we suspect it's also geographically fixed, that is, the side of the bed, at home or abroad. We don't even know why my side has always been on the right and Maralys' on the left. Was it an anatomic predilection? A visual orientation? Or just an accident that created a habit?

There are definite preferences at the dinner table, too. Right-handed or left-handed? Deaf on one side? Preferring an end or edge to avoid crowding? Or seeking the center of action and attention, the middle?

Personality traits and physical impairments come into play, probably unconsciously in most cases. In my case, I opt for an end because I like space and a panoramic view of the group. Maralys, on the other hand, being far more gregarious, gravitates to the center of the action.

The next time you attend a public meeting of

limited duration, you may simply select a seat that's nearby and reasonably accessible. Hopefully on or near the edge.(We never go deep into the middle except for show biz season assigned seats).

But if the meeting reconvenes after a break, or after lunch, see if you try to return to your prior seat. And aren't completely pleased if some less geographically gifted person took it...

Just a suggestion. Maybe you don't have seat orientation or seat envy. Maybe it's only present in professional sitters like me....

2/16/15

Shame Is not my Thing, but...

Is it just me or do all octogenarians wish they had given their parents more attention in their declining years? I had remarkable and diametrically opposite parents who were proud of me as a successful only child, and who lived nearby until they expired in their nineties.

What bothers me now from time to time is how seldom I saw them in those lonely, detached final years when all their friends and relatives were long dead and my family was all they had. My dad, a retired Navy Commander and high school teacher, outlived all four of his brothers and lived a continent away from their offspring. He died at 92.

My mother outlived all six of her siblings and had no nieces or nephews that we knew about. She outlived my dad by five years and died at 94 after years of severe osteoarthritis and spinal stenosis.

I owed both of them for seventy years of support and admiration, yet saw them infrequently in those last ten years, even though their apartment was two miles away from this headquarters. Dad was feeble and deaf.

Mother was barely ambulatory, lonely, and wanting to "go home," although she exhibited "granny" enthusiasm and generosity with her grandchildren in this area.

I have few regrets about my activity during my first 87 years, but seeing so little of Art and Ruth during those painful final years is a big one. I don't know shame as an emotion, but I would have to conclude that my deep regret over neglecting those two faithful forebears during that last decade of their lives is tinged with some shame.

The fact that I was still running a law firm in those twilight years is no excuse for my filial neglect because I wasn't working evenings and we were only two miles apart. I owed them more than I gave them when they needed it most. And there's nothing I can do about it.

They must have wondered about their ungrateful only child at the end, but they never expressed any such disappointment or resentment. They were uncomplaining to the end.

If I believed in an afterlife, I would relay my regrets and tell them how often, and how increasingly, I remember their remarkable accomplishments –through the Depression, through the War, and through the Postwar Era — and their benevolent compromise between two disparate personalities. And their dedication to me and my family. I wish I had thanked and admired them more, verbally and in person. This is one of those areas where there's no second chance.

3/5/15

Protesters, Activists, and Occupiers: Thanks, but No Thanks....

I FULLY UNDERSTAND THE frustration and impatience that leads firm believers to action. They have come to the conclusion that the so-called democratic process — the vote, the phone call, and the letter or petition — are going to produce zero change, whether the issue be wealth disparity or campaign finance or corporate management or Wall Street maneuvering, or abortions. They feel that the only way to create political, corporate, or social pressure for change is to create some hubbub or commotion and get the media cameras and microphones on the scene.

The believers carry posters or banners. The organizers carry bullhorns, lead chants, and reach for media microphones. They are as vocal as they are passionate. They congregate in groups as large as possible and either campaign verbally with passers by or try to block their passage, even in vehicles.

These tactics have led to a plethora of laws and

ordinances designed to prevent pedestrian and vehicle blockage, and to otherwise try to prevent a public nuisance from noise or harassment. But the activists always have the right arm of First Amendment lawyers, who insist that even obnoxious speech or conduct can't be impeded very much.

There are myriad court cases involving issues of criminal trespass or false imprisonment ("Occupiers"). Others involve ordinances designed to limit physical blockage (e.g. abortion clinics, factories) or personal assault by aggressive "activists."

Then there are contests over the ancient common law concept of "public nuisance," usually involving excessive noise or unruly crowds or blocking of traffic or pedestrians.

When we see the ever-more-frequent standoffs between police and activists, we are watching a battle between angry citizens (and hooligan wannabes), and our hired guardians of public order, the police or National Guard. Our American forefathers recognized the risk of mob rule and anarchy, but then loosened the reins of government with the First and Fourteenth Amendments. So the American way was to be a compromise between government power and individual freedom of action.

Historically, I guess our sympathies are supposed to be with the angry mob — witness the civil rights movement — but the faces and tactics of protesters and activists bring out a primordial conservative streak in me, just as I might have been a Loyalist in 1776, despite the stupidity of George III. Sort of the Crown versus the pillagers reaction … The American rebels turned out to be right, or so it seems.

Had I lived in Virginia in 1861, I suspect I would have been sympathetic with the Confederate cause, which, ironically, was anti-government in effect. Yet when I see a standoff between BLM agents and Federal officers versus armed anti-government "militiamen" and tax-dodging "sovereign" freaks, I hated to see the Feds back away to avoid bloodshed.

So I can't figure out where my psyche lies. I was a typical pro-government Orange County Republican conservative until I saw Ronald Reagan as a charismatic phony who knew nothing of history or economics, yet was credited with bringing down an already crumbling Soviet Union. Since Ronnie I've been a Democrat at the polls, but wary of the party line. But when it comes to an angry mob of torch bearers, bull horns, window smashers, and tire burners, I somehow rejoin my Wills forebears as a Taft Republican who scorns public furor and civil disobedience as a prelude to a riot.

I vote "no" on rape, plunder, pillage and burn every time. No rebel here. I'm obviously too comfortable with the status quo….

4/17/15

What the Pot Peddlers Don't Tell You

THE MARIJUANA INITIATIVE PROPONENTS in California tell the public that pot is a lovely alternative to alcohol and nicotine for calming a tense, frenetic, or ailing American public. No tars or toxins, no nasty addiction. The Feds and cops are just uninformed and out of date in regarding marijuana as harmful or addictive.

What the advocates ignore, or have never read, are results of a few long term studies that demonstrate damage to certain portions of the adolescent brain that affect drive and memory. The researchers are now focusing on specific portions of the juvenile brain and are alarmed at what they're seeing.

I'm still waiting for brain researchers to confirm what Maralys and I observed anecdotally back in the pot hazy Seventies, when Nancy Reagan was offering "Just Say No" as the solution to the drug epidemic. If they start dissecting the brains of as many homeless Vietnam vets as they are dissecting from aging pro

171

football players (for CTE), my commencement address condemning marijuana long ago at my high school academy will be vindicated. Stay tuned.

But what the pot promoters fail to mention is the disastrous effect California pot growers are having in Northern California forests, where they farm thousands of acres of cleared forest areas in remote portions of the National and State forests. A Senior Environmental Scientist in the California Department of Fish and Game recently described what nobody sees except by helicopter, but which will have a disastrous long term effect on California's environment.

The marijuana is grown both by international cartels, using illegals as labor, and by domestic opportunists willing to take risks for a chance to get rich. They clear a remote tract that is visible only by air, then they portal in chemicals and fertilizers and plastic pipe. They set up a lab and a watering system that taps, and often drains, a nearby stream. Their fertilizing and water distribution systems are virtually high tech, not DIY or amateur operations.

Ninety five per cent of the California pot farmers are apparently stealing the water without obtaining State permits and the dried up streams no longer support salmon or steelhead trout, hence the involvement of the Fish and Wildlife Department, as well as County Sheriffs. The effect on migrating salmon and trout will be permanent, especially with the current drought already shrinking the watersheds radically.

The streams that pot growers don't drain completely are being polluted by fertilizer runoff and by grading intrusion. The lethal effects are being recorded in the larger rivers downstream, like the Sacramento and San Joaquin rivers. Nothing to lose sleep over, but even the Delta smelt are disappearing because of upstream pollution. What I would lose sleep over would be the complete wipe out of Humboldt and Mendocino salmon and steelhead trout.

Jerry Brown and the Legislature are aware of the crisis. The California Fish and Game Department has a new Watershed Enforcement Team. The California Water Resources Control Board has added new people to address the problem. And hopefully the northern County Sheriffs Departments aren't all on the payroll of the growers and will continue to break up the pot farms by helicopter raids.

We don't even have unity of thinking about the marijuana movement in this family. Some of the next two generations think MJ is a relatively harmless drug that is easily preferable to nicotine and even alcohol. With the already heavy cost of alcohol and tobacco consumption in the U.S., all we need is another mind-altering drug in the workplace and on the highways. Get to work neurologists, physiologists, and psychiatrists! Your long term studies are long overdue....

4/18/15

About the Author

ROBERT V. WILLS TRAVELED extensively as a youth because of a Naval Officer father and a travel-prone mother. Multiplicity also characterized his college years, resulting in three degrees after four universities. His final degree was in Law at UCLA. That led to two different legal careers, one as General Counsel and Officer of a Big Board corporation and the second as a medical malpractice trial lawyer with his own law firm in Southern California.

His first book, *Lawyers are Killing America*, was a plea for genuine tort reform in the U.S. His next volume, *A View From the Hill*, contains essays on myriad areas of the American social and political landscape, reflecting a unique and unorthodox perspective on the passing parade. This volume continues that process.

If you enjoyed the book, please consider leaving a review at the online book seller's page for the book.